Beca

His Glory

A Miraculous Spiritual Journey

Because I've Seen His Glory

His Glory

A Miraculous Spiritual Journey

By Wayne Warmack

~~ CREDITS ~~

Executive Advisor: Sandy Warmack

Cover: Sherri Shipman

Editing/Formatting:

Darlene Jones Beall and Sherri Shipman

Photos: Wayne and Sandy Warmack

X-ray photos by permission: Patrick Keating

ISBN: 9798379341749

CONTENTS

~~ INTRODUCTION ~~

Before presenting this narrative, I feel strongly that I need to explain why I wrote it. This has always amazed me because I've never been what the world would call a successful person. Any number of times ordinary people just like me have approached me and said something like, "Wayne, you really need to write about your experiences." However, recently a prophet named Phillip Rich addressed me personally in one of his services and told me, "You have a mandate from God to write a book about your experiences". In wide-eyed wonder, I nodded my head in the affirmative and promised that I would. Some weeks later we heard that Phil was going to be back in our area. We enjoy his ministry enormously, so we always go if we can.

Since he had delivered that prophetic message to me, I had puzzled over how to start something like that and what to call it that won't sound mundane. I didn't want to disappoint Phil if he asked me whether I had started writing my book. Therefore, I went ahead and started typing, and a virtual torrent of memories started pouring out into this text. Now I had some pages finished the next time I saw Phil so I wouldn't be ashamed of my lazy self.

I sincerely hope you draw something good from my reminiscences. Some last names have been left out of this writing on purpose for various good reasons.

God Bless You!

~~ FOREWORD ~~

Having composed two movements of perhaps the most heart-searching music ever written, Franz Schubert decided to switch his attention from his "unfinished" 8ᵗʰ symphony to one that is nearly endless. Sometimes one's life seems like that, but it's really only a moment of time, a wisp of quickly vanishing vapor – something to make the most of while you can. Because too soon you will have to move from this dressing room into whatever comes next... and you don't want to be improperly attired when it happens.

They are not long,

The days of Wine & Roses,

Out of a Misty Dream

Our Path Emerges for a Little While,

And then it Closes Within a Dream.

~Ernest Dowson~

NEARLY DEAD EXPERIENCE #1

One day in 1956 a young boy, only twelve years of age, peddled a bicycle furiously in the fiercely torrid coastal Texas summer heat from his home to a public swimming pool several miles away. Quickly after arriving, the overheated boy plunged into the cold water of the pool, a mistake he would soon regret.

Immediately situating himself on the steps at the shallow end of the pool, he positioned his diving mask on his forehead and was in process of donning his swim fins when suddenly he experienced something that felt like a mule kick to his small chest. He felt his heart stop, and he immediately slumped over into blackness, face-down in the water, still and apparently lifeless.

Some indeterminate time afterward, his young friend who had accompanied him to the public swimming pool in Pasadena, Texas noticed him floating face-down in the water and gave him a poke in the ribcage. Knowing that his friend was ticklish, and not getting a response from that action, my friend Buddy Lance summoned a lifeguard to help him pull his unresponsive friend out of the water.

The next thing I knew I came around to find myself lying on wet concrete, totally blind, with many excited voices around me and unseen people doing oddly unfamiliar things to my body. I drew a deep agonized breath and began to sob, frightened and not understanding what was going on. An ambulance ride home and a few days later some vision gradually returned to my chlorine-scalded eyes. Soon afterward I got my first pair of eyeglasses for somewhere near normal vision.

That was one of three very close encounters I've had with death. I've heard and read that people having near-death experiences see light at the end of a tunnel, fields of flowers, departed loved ones, angels, and such as that. If I did, I wasn't permitted to recall it. However, the experience left me changed somehow, and permanently not of this world. I began to feel especially alien to its popular culture and its conventionalities, resulting in a separated and uncomfortably misfit life.

GIFTINGS

From an early age, I had a gift for absorbing both useful and trivial knowledge, but I was a far below-average achiever in public school. I was disinterested in its curricula, and I rarely finished assignments. This resulted in three years of 8th grade, many sessions of summer school, and a very late and unceremonious graduation from high school at the age of nineteen. I was considered slightly retarded, but all that time I was teaching myself to play the violin, composing classical music, and teaching myself elements of several foreign languages.

That can spawn a runaway ego if one does not understand that these abilities are gifts given by a gracious and overseeing creator God and not merely clever inventions of one's own mind. The giver of the gifts then watches patiently to see what that one will do with their gifts. Will they be used to glorify Him, or will they be used to glorify their self to further their selfish ambitions? It takes many years and many bitter experiences to gain the wisdom to make the appropriate decision about that.

MY FIRST 'CELLO

I was 14 years of age when I asked my dad to buy me a violin. I felt a strong love for the sound of the instrument. My parents were good providers but of a very humble station in life. Dad didn't take my request very seriously.

I had an inexpensive guitar that he had bought for me some years before, but I couldn't get interested in it. I didn't learn how to do much with it until one day I had the inspiration to fashion a bow for it and improvise a high wooden bridge on it that would enable it to be played somewhat like a violoncello. That convinced my dad that I was serious, and he rented me a violin. I eventually restored the guitar and gifted it to my first daughter some years later.

Dad then subscribed me to a correspondence course in violin playing from the U.S. School of Music in Port Washington NY, and I took off teaching myself to play the violin. It couldn't have been very pleasant listening to my early scrapings on the thing. Soon afterward I was playing in the middle school orchestra. Before too long I had won an audition for the first chair in the All-District Orchestra in the Pasadena, Texas school system. I took a few helpful lessons from some local string teachers, but I was mostly self-taught.

I practiced diligently, grinding my way through all the recommended books of violin Etudes, but I never really excelled on the instrument enough to become a skillful and competent soloist. I simply lacked the encouragement or discipline to go that far. That shortcoming has marked my life to this very day. I had always been satisfied with mediocrity in myself - just good enough to stay in the game.

That is NOT a virtue!

In those days I habituated Paul Buskirk's music store in my hometown of Pasadena (the real one, in Texas), where I hoped to absorb some musical knowledge by osmosis. I'm not sure I ever did that. However, I did learn from Paul that they can't grow sunflowers in Alaska because in the summer the sun goes around in circles and twists their heads off.

Paul claimed to have been the inventor of the double-neck guitar. He's long since passed away, but you can find Paul Buskirk on old YouTube videos.

STUDIO ORCHESTRA

As a young adult in the 1970s, I did have the privilege of being hired for several years as a violinist in a recording studio orchestra in Houston's Ludwig Sound Studio. They employed an arranger and specialized in recording Christian groups who sang what was then called inspirational songs. That genre of Christian music featured lush orchestrations and gorgeous lofty melodies that have sadly disappeared.

That was where I came in as one of four violinists alongside a 'cello and two French horns. We laid down multiple tracks for Charles Ludwig, which when combined sounded very much like a substantially larger orchestra. I did that for several years until I finally left the Houston area in the 1980s.

COLLEGE

Out of high school in 1964, I took a music scholarship to Sam Houston State University in Huntsville, Texas as a violin and composition major. I was told that the institution was originally called the Sam Houston Institute of Technology. I don't know whether that's true or not, but apparently, nobody wanted to wear the letter jackets, so they changed the name. I stayed there for two semesters, but generally lacking ambition I dropped out and got married.

I married a beautiful young woman I had met there. It was a great move for me, but not for her as I was lacking in moral character. Jesus had not yet made inroads into my life. She should have stayed in school and got her diploma and a real life.

We stayed together long enough to raise two fine beautiful daughters. Then I eventually made that bad moral choice that has brought emotional and spiritual devastation to countless marriages. It was many years before my daughters could bring themselves to have a civil relationship with me again.

MA BELL & HOLY GHOST

The first job I took right after the marriage began was as a lineman for Southwestern Bell Telephone Company. Back then employees called the company "Ma Bell." That lasted about six months. A young man who is deathly afraid of heights has no business climbing telephone poles.

However, during that brief and largely unpleasant experience, I found myself a captive audience to a good Pentecostal gentleman at about 30 feet above the ground for several hours a day during those months. His title was Cable Splicer and mine was Cable Splicer's Helper. I learned some skills up there on those poles that have served me well a few times since then.

Bob Townsend was from Vidor, Texas and he drilled a lot of Pentecostal doctrine into me up there. He also convinced me of my need for a savior and a baptism in the Holy Ghost, and how much joy it would bring me.

Looking back at the age of twelve, shortly before the drowning incident, I had answered a Baptist altar call in Tampa Florida, the city of my 1944 birth. The sermon was delivered by an evangelist cousin of mine by the name of Willis Kirk and his impassioned message reached my tender young heart for Jesus. From then, until I grew up, I had not thought much about it. I assumed that's all there was to it; just going to the front of the church and saying "I do" to Jesus. Now it was 1965 and at an old-fashioned wooden altar in that Pentecostal church in Pasadena Texas, I received a Holy Spirit baptism, and it truly was ecstatic.

SALVATION WITHOUT DISCIPLESHIP

We remained members of that congregation for ten years, getting ten solid years of indoctrination in Pentecostal dogma and not a whole lot else. We also learned to fear God as a glowering and angry being who was poised to strike us with something frightful if we didn't keep our hair and clothing just so, if we went to a movie, wore jewelry, wore facial hair or make-up, or looked at television.

We learned that God was a terrifying and vengeful creature who was always on the verge of launching his temper in our general direction. That's no way to disciple a believer to prepare him or her for the daunting issues of life on this demon-infested rock.

What we didn't get during those ten years was the precious truth that God is a loving Daddy who wants to have a warm, intimate, and nurturing relationship with his children, even within the confines of some exacting expectations. Without that knowing, a believer is kept stunted in his or her faith and is potentially morally weak.

Don't get me wrong, I'm not blaming anyone else for my subsequent moral failures. Although we did see it happen to others in that church many times during those years and at that time we didn't understand why.

HERE COME THE CHARISMANIACS

In the early 1970s, the Charismatic Renewal was beginning to sweep the nation from its conspicuous beginnings in the Los Angeles area among The Jesus People. We were eventually invited to attend some gatherings in the garage of an ancient house near downtown Houston which had been established as a Christian coffee house called The Way In. They featured a folk-style acoustic-only instrumental and singing group called The Keyhole.

The Way In was a ministry of a rather large Anglican church in downtown Houston called Church of The Redeemer. Something wonderful had begun to happen at that church. The Holy Spirit had invaded Redeemer with tongues, other spiritual gifts, and also with much joy, resulting in a level of worship there and at the coffee house such as we had never seen or heard before as Pentecostals.

The songs had a distinctly folk flavor to them with definite old English modal characteristics. The vinyl record albums that the Way In group recorded during those days are still available for listening and archived on the YouTube video website. It's quite a wonderful experience hearing them for the first time. Most of the songs were composed by members of the Church of The Redeemer in Houston, and they breathe life in such a way as perhaps has not been heard again since the 1970s.

The outstanding characteristic of the Way In coffee house and its attendees was spontaneously joyful outpourings of genuine compassionate love, which characterized the entire Charismatic Renewal of those days. We were swept off our feet by it, for such was rarely seen in the fault-finding church we had been attending.

When it got back to the pastor and other members of our church that we had been sneaking off to these Friday evening gatherings at the Way In, a coffee house in that garage in downtown Houston, we were sternly warned, "Those people are not saved, and you shouldn't be going there!"

Of course, "not saved" meant they were not part of our denomination or ("demon-imation", as one insightful pastor called them). However, we continued going as often as we could, because the Charismatic love bug had bitten us, and it felt so right!

NOT A D.J.

In 1969, just previous to our immersion into the Charismatic movement, I had stumbled onto becoming a radio announcer (not a DJ) at a classical radio station in Houston - KLEF-FM. I had grown weary of my job as an Auxiliary Dynamo Operator at the Deepwater Electric Generating Station, a facility of Houston Lighting & Power Company.

It was rotating shift work, and much of the time it was a very lonely, boring, and, especially at night, sleepy job in an atmosphere of very loud noise, heat, humidity, and an over-abundance of the Texas gulf coast's official state bird, the Aedes Aegypti mosquito. It is alleged that they have been known to carry off small children, but I'm not a witness to that. What led me into a radio career that was to last more than a quarter century was another bit of serendipity, of which there were yet to be many more in my life.

DON'T LAUGH

You might recall that I became a paid violinist after enrolling in a correspondence course. Well, here we go again! Somebody told me I had a nice speaking voice, so I enrolled in the (don't laugh!) the Columbia School of Broadcasting correspondence course.

When I got my first lesson assignment, they told me to go visit my favorite radio station in order to see what goes on in one. To make a long story short, the program director hired me on the spot, launching me into a twenty-seven-year career in radio broadcasting.

Radio didn't pay much in the particular field of broadcasting that I stumbled into, but it was fun and emotionally rewarding, for maybe about a week and a half. I was soon to realize that a radio station can be one of the loneliest outposts on earth, and it all becomes a dreary and repetitive routine after a while.

The broadcasting school correspondence course, oh, I finally finished that. I'm sure I was considered a prodigy by my instructors who had never met me.

It's just 'way too easy to fake your way through life
if you're clever enough!

After working at KLEF-FM, a classical music station, for a few months, I heard about an opening for an announcer (in Britain it is called a "presenter") at a very prestigious Beautiful Music radio station in one of the most opulent neighborhoods in Houston. I auditioned at KODA and was immediately hired. In the ensuing years, I was to have many more part-time fill-in jobs at KLEF, but this new experience at KODA AM/FM radio was the beginning of many very wonderful, and sometimes incredibly funny experiences at one of the most illustrious radio stations that has ever graced any American city.

HONEY **SNIFF**

I had been mostly a classical music snob in my formative years, and I had never heard many current popular songs on purpose. At KODA, part of my job was to produce commercial spot announcements when required, and something I excelled in, which was pre-recording a five-minute newscast every hour.

While the pre-recorded newscast was playing from the FM automation system, I was charged with intercepting the Mutual Broadcasting System Network news for the AM station, which was in the same building, with a live station ID and time check. Sometimes pulling this off skillfully got frantic, and a good pair of track shoes helped a lot.

One day another staff announcer who wasn't busy at the time volunteered to engineer the AM network news break so I could do a live newscast and weather on the FM station. I was poised at the microphone in the FM studio with my headset on and waiting for the last song to play out just before pausing the automated music system and going into live news at the top of the hour. That's when I began to listen to the song that was playing in my headphones. A fatal mistake!

It was a thing I had never heard before by a fellow named Bobby Goldsboro, and it was called "Honey". I don't want to go too much into what the song was about, but here I am in the news booth at Houston's most prestigious radio station with a listenership of hundreds of thousands, and I'm seconds away from starting a live newscast, and I'm crying like a baby because of what happened to "Honey" in this stupid song! I couldn't stop blubbering. I had to literally throw off my headphones, dash out of the studio, and summon the program director to come quickly to read the news for me because I'm uncontrollably choking on tears!

He dashed into the news booth and got the headphones on at precisely the instant that the song ended. He threw the microphone switch and read the news for me with a big smile on his face, trying hard not to laugh! Do you realize that you can actually hear a smile on the radio? Smiles don't go well with international tensions and local police reports.

That extraordinary gentleman's name was James Rhett Butler, and he was one of the most lovable and unforgettable characters I have ever had the privilege of knowing. I could tell you so much more about my experiences there! We called him Rhett, and I got the news recently that he had preceded me to Heaven. I can hardly wait to greet him with a hug when I get there.

A CHILDHOOD HERO

Let me just touch on another of the most remarkable things about my years at KODA AM/FM radio. As a child, I had grown up listening to two fabulous voices on a local Beautiful Music AM radio station called KXYZ. These were staff announcer Milton Willis and the station manager Fred Nahas. I drank of these beautiful voices on the radio as if they were expensive champagne, never dreaming that someday I would actually meet them and work alongside them. They were both working at KODA when I was hired there, and I was awestruck by this good fortune.

Milton Willis was my broadcasting mentor, and I always did strive to sound like him in his absolutely perfect diction and voice modulation. He was a very funny and gentle fellow with the most elegant radio voice you or I have ever heard, even to this day decades later. The only other radio voice I ever wanted to sound like was the incomparable Bill Pearce of the Night Sounds syndicated radio broadcasts in the latter part of the past century.

Both Milton and Bill have passed on to their rewards. [Re-broadcasts of Bill Pearce's Night Sounds broadcasts can still be heard on the internet. Treat yourself!

LAKEWOOD

In 1975 some friends convinced us to visit Lakewood International Outreach Center, pastored by the late John Osteen. There again we found that oasis of love that we had been longing for, just like at the Way In, except much bigger. After ten years of holiness Pentecostal indoctrination, we couldn't figure out how these "unsaved" people could be so full of joy and obvious love for each other, for Jesus, and even for us. And the miracles we began seeing there...! We persisted in visiting that wonderful church, and in 1975 we eventually disappeared from our previous church in Pasadena, Texas.

One of the sweetest memories I have about the Charismatic church movement at that time was the songs! They were absolutely lovely musical inventions comprised of Bible passages from the King James Version, sung with sweet and expressive melodies. At Lakewood Church in Houston, the song leader didn't tell you to turn to a such-and-such song in a hymn book. He told you to turn to a such-and-such passage of scripture in your KJV bible and sing it with him. It was WONDERFUL! It had a glorious sweetness about it!

A CURSE AND A BLESSING

Earlier that year, I had begun to experience debilitating back pain from the physical stress of handling washing machines while working as a service technician for Sears-Roebuck & Co. In 1975 I went to a hospital in a suburb of Houston, Pasadena, Texas for surgery.

While lying on my back in pain and waiting to be taken into surgery for the procedure, the pastor of the Pentecostal church we no longer attended came sternly into the room, shook his finger in my face, and pronounced a devil's curse on me for leaving the church. I won't go into any details about what began to happen to him almost immediately after he did that. I still believe he was really a very good man but was blinded by denominational prejudice. I held no hard feelings, because of the new love relationship with Jesus I had found at the original Lakewood in Houston.

Later that same afternoon the Lakewood pastor, John Osteen, came into my hospital room, smiled, laughed, and joked with me, and prayed a sincere prayer and a blessing over me. The surgery went extremely well, and I have had no more back problems since then. However, after the surgery, I had no feeling in half of my left hand which includes the pinkie finger and the ring finger. I mentioned the problem to absolutely no one, not even my wife, assuming that it would eventually go away.

30

THAT HAND

The following Christmas season I was asked to sing Stille Nacht, Heilige Nacht (Silent Night) in German at Lakewood Church which served many international cultures. I positioned myself on the platform behind Pastor Osteen, waiting for him to finish giving announcements preparatory to my song.

Suddenly he paused in mid-sentence, was briefly silent for a few seconds as though listening to something or someone, and then still facing away from me he said, "That hand is going to be all right now." Then he immediately continued with what he had been saying before. It did not occur to me right away what had happened, but as I was stepping down after singing my song and returning to my seat, I suddenly noticed that sensation had returned to my entire left hand!

John Osteen was a true God's General, and my few years at the original Lakewood International Outreach Center in Houston were days of glory.

THE CAMERONS FROM SCOTLAND

This Lakewood story is in order here: There was a visiting Scottish missionary family, the Camerons who came to Lakewood to minister to us in song and the Word of God while we were there. Simon Cameron, the daddy of the family, mounted the podium after being introduced and announced to the congregation in his magnificent Scottish brogue how pleased he was to be at the...."Layeckwude Inter-r-r-rnational Outr-r-r-reach Center-r-r".

After he said that John Osteen stepped forward, put his hand gently on Simon's shoulder, and said, "Aw shoot, Simon, just say Lakewood Church so you don't hafta trill all them Rs". Incidentally, Papa Simon Cameron was the composer of this joyful song...

THE DANCING HEART
"Oh, the Holy Ghost will set your feet a-dancing.
The Holy Ghost will thrill you through and through.
The Holy Ghost will set your feet a-dancing,
And set your heart a-dancing too!"

That was an enormously popular standard in the Charismatic realm for many years. You just never knew what was going to happen at Lakewood. It was rarely boring because Jesus and angels were there IN MANIFESTATION.

ABIDING ANOINTING OF FAVOR

The old original Lakewood Church on East Houston Road on the northeast side of town was full of beautiful signs, wonders, miracles, intoxicating joy, and holy glory while John Osteen was the pastor. On the grounds behind the building, there was a room-sized concrete pad surmounted by a pole-barn style roof which sheltered a picnic table and a beverage vending machine. At night this shelter was illuminated by a single dangling light bulb, and we would often pause there for light conversation and a bit of refreshment before heading home.

I shall never forget one late Wednesday evening, when I was feeding coins into the Coke machine with family and friends, when a well-dressed young gentleman walked out of the darkness, purposefully approached me, introduced himself as Tom, and said, "Sir, the Lord wants you to know that he has placed upon you an Abiding Anointing of Favor." I didn't really understand what that meant, but I thanked him kindly for the message. Upon that, he turned around, walked out into the darkness, and disappeared. I was to eventually begin to understand what that signified as events continued to unfold in my rather insignificant life.

LOCKSMITH

One of the manifestations of "An Abiding Anointing Of Favor" that I began to experience along the way in the 1970s was when for some reason I became fascinated with locks and keys and how they work. Having heard somewhere that locksmiths earn awesome incomes, I enrolled in the (don't laugh!) the Belsaw School of Locksmithing correspondence course.

Let me tell you right now, a little knowledge can get you into some awfully tight situations, which with my minuscule correspondence course knowledge I quickly began to get into. However, I soon acquired enough understanding from some old pros, that I equipped myself and got into the business of picking locks and making keys when there was no original key to make it from.

Inebriated persons who had lost their car keys in dark parking lots outside of bars became some of my best customers. I continued in that part-time profession until I moved from Houston to another state in 1984. My last four years in professional locksmithing were spent as an institutional locksmith at The University of Texas Health Science Center in Houston. Lots of interesting experiences there too!

HEY! STORE THIS FOR ME!

During the wonderful Charismatic Renewal of the 1970s, I became acquainted with a loving large family of ardent believers who comprised the Day family. Francis and Patsy Day, along with their 4 sons, were the most hospitable, caring, loving, and selfless people I have ever met to this day. I and my family quickly became part of their family, and their home became our home during visits.

Their philosophy about their home was, "Don't knock and don't ask. Just come on in and enjoy anything we have." They lived very modest lives in Channelview Texas, near Houston, and were to be my very closest and dearest friends for thirty years.

A homeward call for Patsy Day in 1999 and later for Francis Day in 2005 ended all of that, and I haven't had a really intimate friend in all the years since then. Francis and I could not have been two more different people, except that "Abiding Anointing Of Favor" was in full manifestation the entire time we were brothers, and it was to give birth to one singularly strange series of events during our relationship.

It began with our mutual acquaintance with a young pastor who had moved to Houston from New Mexico and rented an old church house on Market Street, near Channelview. While inspecting the vacant building, Francis and Pastor Gary Wood came upon a derelict vintage 1947 Kay® Double-Bass in a closet. For those of you who do not know what a double-bass is, it's a 'cello with a pituitary problem. It's often called a stand-up bass or a bull fiddle. With the C-extension added later and the end-pin extended, this one stood about seven feet tall.

Francis Day negotiated with Pastor Gary Wood and bought that bass fiddle from the church for $50. Then, Francis shoved it at me and said, "Hey, store this for me." Francis Day was a prophet, and he knew I would be using it later to help support my family with it.

Well, I took that giant fiddle and "stored it" for Francis Day for the rest of his life and far beyond that. I was eventually to return the favor 38 years later when I asked somebody else to store it for me! That's another story for another time.

36

Soon after receiving the instrument, I somehow purchased a bow for it and began to try figuring out how to play the darn thing. Not many days later I heard about a volunteer orchestra in the area, got the conductor's name and number, and I audaciously called him, "Hi, I'm a bass player. Do you mind if I come and attend a rehearsal?" (I exaggerated only a little!)

He was overjoyed, and said, "Come on!" He didn't even ask, "How long have you been playing?", or the typical classical snob question "Under WHOM did you study?" He just said, "Come on!" based on careless assumptions that I actually knew how to play the darn thing. That began a 38-year career in playing that double bass in many symphony orchestras in many cities while I was "storing it" for Francis Day.

Oh, yes, I finally did catch on to how to play it.

MORE ABOUT GARY WOOD

Sometime in the latter part of the 1970s I and my family and the Day family became busy with a church in Pasadena (the real one, in Texas), called Abundant Life. This was a fellowship in full manifestation of joyful Charismatic renewal.

One Sunday morning the congregation was introduced to the new associate pastor, Mr. Gary Wood, newly relocated to our area from Hobbs, New Mexico. On his inaugural morning at Abundant Life, we had a supernatural visitation that was obviously intended by the Holy Spirit to reassure Gary that he was in the right place at the right time.

Immediately after song service and magnificent corporate praise were winding down, a very big man who was known to be a little mentally retarded got up out of his seat in the auditorium, stepped to the open aisle, and began to execute a Native American war dance in the aisle while he chanted something like, "Hee-yuh hai-yuh ee-yeh hai-yuh hee-yuh ee-yeh, etc." for about one whole minute. He then quietly sat down and there fell a tense silence in the room.

A few seconds later, a lady member of the worship team spoke an interpretation, and it was about the deep, deep love of Jesus and more. A few seconds later Gary Wood stood up from his seat with tears streaming down his face, went to the podium, and said, "As a little child I grew up playing with the Navajo children on the reservation in New Mexico, and I learned their language. What that lady said just now in English is exactly what that man down there sang in the Navajo language."

Talk about an endorsement! I'll never forget that day! [Search: "It's Supernatural, Gary Wood" on YouTube.]

LAUGHTER IN THE HOLY SPIRIT

You might remember the extremely controversial manifestation of laughter that characterized the time of spiritual refreshing we had in the 1990s. On one particular Sunday evening meeting at Abundant Life in Pasadena (the REAL one, in Texas), one attractive middle-aged woman who was not given to foolishness began to laugh uncontrollably during corporate prayer. Nobody was bothered by it because it quickly became contagious, and we welcomed the Holy Spirit in that place.

Because her joyful laughter wasn't allowing her space to breathe, even though she was having the best time of her life. So were we, observing her! She began gasping out, "Shut it off, Lord, shut it off!" Spiritually it was blessing and cleansing her, but physically it was more than she could handle. Gradually it began to subside, and she began to breathe again. Afterward, she had the most peacefully rapturous look on her pretty tear-stained face that you could ever imagine.

There is a remarkable difference between holy laughter in the Holy Spirit and the faked laughter or even demonic laughter which sounds sardonic and NOT happy. I've heard both! When it's of God it is happy and healing and holy and REAL.

If you are praying for revival, what you get might not be what you wanted. Revival is not what happens when a preacher shows up. Revival is what happens when God shows up and does what He jolly well pleases. It almost always offends the denominational folks because it's out of character with their prideful religious dignity.

MIGRATION

Having been born to Wayne E. and Marion Warmack at Drew Field US Army airbase in Tampa, Florida in 1944, and raised from age five in Houston and Pasadena, Texas, I got an uncontrollable wilderness itch in 1984. As a result, I moved myself and my unwilling family to the Ozark mountain country of northwestern Arkansas.

Shortly before our move, an ancient rural house near Lincoln, Arkansas was secured for us by my then-father-in-law, a very kind gentleman who had settled in the area with his wife a short time earlier. He had retired as an overseas executive with a well-known oil company. The house he found for us had previously been the post office in the tiny farming community of Rhea's Mill near Lincoln.

I don't know whether it was really God's will for me to drag my family from the economic security of Houston, Texas to Arkansas. My two girls were extremely unhappy with this move. Also, for the ensuing six years, I went into a steep spiritual, moral, and mental decline which I still believe would not have happened had I stayed in Houston. I began to experience darkly seductive spiritual forces in Arkansas such as I had never known in Texas, and I stupidly allowed them to do their nasty work in me.

FIRST JOBS IN ARKANSAS

Soon after getting settled in Arkansas in the summer of 1984, I was hired as an announcer at an Easy Listening radio station (KEZA-FM) in the tall First Place building on the beautiful downtown square in Fayetteville. Only a few days afterward, I arranged for an audition with the then-conductor of the North Arkansas Symphony Orchestra in Fayetteville. The music director, Dr. Carlton Woods admitted that he really didn't know how to audition a bassist, so I played a piece for him that I had written, and easily passed that audition. That same day I signed a contract as one of the half dozen or so contra-bassists in the North Arkansas Symphony Orchestra.

Maestro Woods was an admirable leader of the orchestra who had the odd habit, after mounting the podium, of pausing, closing his eyes, and then tapping himself on the forehead several times before lifting his baton. He would then smile pleasantly at his orchestra and give the downbeat for the glorious music to begin. I had many wonderful and happy experiences with that orchestra until it went out of business early in the new century due to some unfortunate decisions having been made by management.

Shortly after being hired by NASO in 1984, the music director of Grand Avenue Baptist Church in Fort Smith called the NASO symphony office in Fayetteville inquiring about the availability of a double-bass player. They gave him my name and number, and I was hired to play in the Grand Avenue Baptist Church orchestra they were putting together for a Christmas cantata. A few days later I made the ninety-mile drive southward over the magnificent Boston Mountains, which are part of the Ozark Mountain Range, to Fort Smith for the rehearsal at the church. I situated myself and my enormous instrument next to the other double-bass player whose name was John Thelman.

John Thelman was a tall, thin, and distinguished gentleman with one of the warmest and most welcoming personalities I have ever encountered. He reminded me very much of Mr. Rogers. After the rehearsals were finished, and then the end of the actual performance, my bass-playing partner John Thelman turned to me and said, "Wayne, I'm the conductor of the Fort Smith Symphony Orchestra, and I'd sure like to have you playing for me."

I was newly arrived in Arkansas with only minimal experience with the instrument and no formal lessons, and very shortly I'm hired by a highly rated radio station and TWO professional symphony orchestras! Don't blame me! It's that "Abiding Anointing Of Favor" thing from Daddy again! I was to remain a well-compensated performing member of the excellent Fort Smith Symphony Orchestra for 33 wonderful years.

DON'T DO IT!

After getting settled in northwestern Arkansas at the age of 39, I was faced with some moral temptations with which I was totally unfamiliar. As a result, I began to slip into sin deeper and deeper and was eventually snared by witchcraft seduction. I also fell victim to my own foolish ego and conceit. Then, due to an unsanctified intimacy, tormenting demons entered into me to reinforce the ones which I believe I had inherited from my deeply disturbed mother.

Gentlemen, if you get involved with a person in an unsanctified physical relationship, you will eventually pay a price in this life that you can't afford. In the midst of one of my forbidden dalliances I DISTINCTLY heard a small and gentle voice say to me,

"SON, YOU ARE BORROWING HAPPINESS FROM TOMORROW AT AN UNBELIEVABLE RATE OF INTEREST."

In the ecstasy of the moment, I chose to ignore that warning. Yes, I eventually repented after the nagging heartache began, and Yes, Jesus is faithful to forgive. But CAN YOU forgive yourself after you have destroyed your marriage and emotionally scarred the precious wife of your youth and your children for the rest of their lives?

Believe me, please; forgiving myself has been the longest and most drawn-out agony of my entire life. You can ask Jesus to pull the nails out of the board, but the nail holes don't heal for a long, long time – if ever.

MEN! If she isn't your wife, DIE TO THAT IMPULSE! Jesus said to take up your CROSS and follow him in holiness. CRUCIFY your flesh and DIE DAILY to those impulses and forbidden desires. Jesus (God) died physically in great agony so that you and I could eventually pass on into the sweet by-and-by at the end of this physical life. But if you don't take up your cross and crucify yourself daily there are painful consequences in the nasty now-and-now too.

Have I made myself perfectly clear?

RESCUED

By the winter of 1990, I had abandoned my family and had moved into a flop-house motel on South School Street in Fayetteville, Arkansas. I was heavily demon-controlled and quite out of my mind due to my various indiscretions having collided with God's perfect will.

That was one of the coldest winters on record in this region, so I bought myself a bottle of strong stuff from the beverage store across the street, turned off the small wall-mounted heater in the room, removed all my clothes, and started consuming the contents of the bottle, hoping to find some release in it from my torments. I was also trying consciously to freeze myself to death in the process.

One very early morning that week, my dearest and only friend in the world, Francis Day, drove 10 hours all night in his pickup truck from Channelview, Texas to Fayetteville, Arkansas to collect the pieces of my life and take them back to his house in Texas.

Francis was a true prophet of God, and God had told Francis the previous evening to go and get me. I did not want to find myself back on the ugly stinking Texas gulf coast with its heat, humidity, mosquitos, and worst of all, thick refinery fumes;

but I was so dissipated and mentally wasted that I was powerless to resist.

A few days after arriving at the Day house in Channelview, a traveling prophet & evangelist in a motor home stopped at the Day house for a brief visit. I do not remember his name and had never seen him before or since. He did not know me, and he knew absolutely nothing about me; but that day, standing on the driveway of the Day house, he spoke to me forthrightly and said, "I see you being taken against your will from the city where you are, to a city where you do not want to be; but it is God's will, and for your good." That gave me considerable comfort, and I knew then that I was somehow starting on a road to recovery of my mind and my soul.

THAT WRONG NUMBER CALL SAVED ME

One day the phone rang at the Day house and Francis picked it up. It was a young Jewish woman named Iris, calling the wrong number from a radio station that I was eventually to work for in downtown Houston. Somehow, she struck up a conversation with Francis, and it turned out that she was a member of a Messianic Jewish congregation in the affluent west side of Houston, of which Channelview is a blue-collar east-side suburb.

Francis and I had both, for many years, been fascinated students of Hebraic culture, and I had already long ago taken courses in Biblical and modern Hebrew, while Francis had long been an avid student of Jewish history and customs. Well, right away we planned to attend the next Saturday morning's Shabbat (Sabbath) service at Congregation Beth Messiah synagogue.

Unlike the few Messianic congregations here in the mid-south, most of the people in this congregation of believers in Yeshua (Jesus) were actually blood-line Jews. There was a radiant glory in this place of a unique type that I had never before experienced, and that holy glory tormented the things which were inside me, bringing copious tears from my eyes.

Aside from the Jewish liturgy which they repeated at each service, they worshipped God in a way I had never before experienced - blowing shofars (rams' horns), singing powerful

Jewish-flavored worship songs in both Hebrew and English, and exuberantly DANCING the Hora in circular groups with their hands linked. There were costumed troupes of well-coordinated dancers doing the Hora in a circle to these gorgeous middle-eastern-sounding Hebrew worship songs. Every time those dancers took the floor and started doing that, I would cry like a baby, because it stirred up some deep emotion like I had been there before and had finally come home. That rented meeting place had a loft overlooking the sanctuary – a literal Upper Room – where those who wished to could assemble before the beginning of the Shabbat service for prayer.

The young Jewish woman who had called the wrong number to Francis Day's house that day was there and bestowed a beautiful old Tallit (prayer covering) on me. Her name was Iris, and she became my intercessor and was very instrumental in my eventual deliverance and recovery. I would go each Saturday morning and worship Yeshua under that Tallit and weep uncontrollably for the sin and torment that was still in my life, but Daddy was beginning to bring me out already.

That Tallit, although I had never even thought of owning one before, felt so comforting and familiar, like I had been under one at some previous time. (Note: I do NOT believe in reincarnation! However, I DO believe in reintarnation. That's when you die and come back as a hillbilly.)

THE SLOB ON THE BACK SEAT

Iris was, and still is, a brilliant and WITTY young lady! One Saturday morning I came into the synagogue wearing a spotlessly clean long-sleeved white shirt that I had taken out of my travel bag that morning. I'm not a particularly fashionable person, so I didn't really notice or even care that the shirt needed some smashing flat. I was sitting on one of the back rows waiting for the service to begin because I didn't feel worthy to take a seat up front, and here comes Iris sashaying briskly down the aisle past me, and without stopping she says, as she passes, really loud, "Hey Wayne, why ya sittin' 'way back here? Ya think that's gonna take the wrinkles outta ya shoit?"

When she said that, the tragedy mask I had been wearing for months crumbled and fell off my face, and I laughed deeply and hilariously for several minutes. That was when something really evil inside me began to get shaken loose. The devils inside me didn't like that place anyhow. I was soon to be informed that the Spirit-filled associate Rabbi, Michael Bryan, and his extraordinary wife, Patricia, were deliverance ministers. They eventually took me on as a challenge and ministered deliverance to me in their living room. There's a lot to say about that some other time, but it was a totally transformational grace experience, and it started re-directing my life.

This messianic Jewish congregation was filled to overflowing with the Holy Spirit, and they exercised the power of God in a measure like I have seldom seen. They are definitely not playing religious games.

JOB FAVOR IN HOUSTON

While in Houston, Jesus provided me with two employments – one was weekdays at an AM Christian news/talk/music radio station. The staff there, including Iris, were deeply committed Spirit-filled believers who had a sweet influence on me in the most wonderful ways. I can't remember the call sign of that station now after all these years, but it was certainly the most wholesome and joyful experience of my entire broadcasting career. The music format was drawn mostly from the Hosanna/Integrity project CDs of that decade.

My job at the station was morning drive-time news, weather, traffic reports, and commercial spot announcements. My weekend radio gig was at KRTS-FM, a classical music station that occupied the entire top penthouse floor of the very tall Cullen Center Tower in downtown Houston. The station was owned, operated, and funded by an extremely wealthy oil tycoon who had a passion for the arts. My vocal abilities and gifts for music history and foreign language phonetics secured me a place there, but very soon I was to return...

BACK TO ARKANSAS

After receiving deliverance that year, 1991, circumstances and a strong inner leading propelled me back to Arkansas in the autumn, recently forgiven, set free from demonic influences, and feeling absolutely invincible in the Lord. When you are feeling invincible - watch out! Because your ancient enemy still has his sights on you, and I guarantee he has traps prepared to spring on you!

In returning to beautiful Arkansas, I had no job and almost no money. All my possessions were in a very small U-Haul trailer following behind me.

Quite soon after arriving back in Arkansas, I got in touch with a radio executive I had worked for in previous years, and coincidentally, while I was in Houston he had been wondering where I was and how he could get in touch with me because he was building an FM easy-listening radio station in Fort Smith, and he wanted me there! In addition to that, I was immediately accepted back into both the Fort Smith Symphony Orchestra and the North Arkansas Symphony Orchestra.

See how Jesus takes care of us if we place full trust in him?

I settled into a small efficiency apartment in Fort Smith with two dollars remaining in my pocket and absolutely nothing else. With most of those two dollars, I was able to purchase one single large heavy loaf of sourdough bread from a local bakery. I rationed pieces of that bread out to myself over the following two weeks until I got my first paycheck from KEZU-FM.

STUMBLING FROM FRYING PAN INTO FIRE

I am convinced that most of us who know Jesus often ignore what he is trying to tell us because we are listening more to our flesh than to Him, so I soon fell for a very pretty Cherokee-Choctaw woman in Fort Smith, and I took her and her young son unto myself in marriage. Some people warned me, but I wasn't willing to listen. So, I unlocked the door to 9 more years of pain and grief when I did that. Hard-headed me was about to take another LONG lap around Mount Sinai.

She and her son had psycho-spiritual baggage that I did not yet know how to deal with, and it almost destroyed me from 1991 to 2001. Early in the year of 1999, I was alone attending a meeting in Tulsa, OK, when a true prophet named Larry Bishop spoke to me by the Holy Spirit, saying "Sir, the Spirit is telling me that you have gotten yourself into a relationship that was not His will for you, and He will soon release you from it." Larry's church is Dove Ministries in Jenks, OK, a Tulsa suburb.

The "soon" turned out to be eighteen more months. I faithfully bore under that misery until one day the Lord Jesus clearly said to me, "Son, you don't need to take any more of this." With the greatest of relief and no sadness, I cut the ties that bound me to that ill-advised relationship. Deliverance number two.

The only regret I have today is that at that time I did not know how to set her and her little boy free from the things that tormented them. Since then, she has been set free and is a very different person now, Praise God! I thought I was mighty in the Lord since receiving my own deliverance.

Sure enough, I had the weapons to set those precious souls free, but I did not yet know how to use them. Discipleship and sound teaching are more important in the life of the believer than you or I can ever fully realize. However, as the scriptures plainly reveal, we can't get it all at once, because...

"To whom would he teach knowledge?
And to whom would he interpret the message?
Those just weaned from the milk?
Those just taken from the breast?
For he says,
Order on Order
Order on Order
Line on Line
Line on Line
A little here
A little there
(...from Isaiah 28)

A PAIN IN THE BUTT

Shortly after that marriage began in 1991, I heard about a radio station that was in the process of being created in the Bella Vista, Arkansas market with a proposed format that I felt like I could live with and work with, and significantly better pay than I was getting in Fort Smith, so we moved from Fort Smith to Rogers, Arkansas which put us within practical driving distance to the station.

I don't remember how we chose Rogers or how we settled on that apartment complex, but I'm sure that Jesus led us there because of events that would soon follow. We went into the office of the apartment managers, Stan and Violet Moroff, to sign the lease papers for the apartment, and after signing, Stan said, "Do you mind if we pray before you leave?" This was a happy discovery that we were renting from believers with a sincere prayer life.

One of the traumatic reactions that I experienced upon the death of my father in 1990, while I was in Houston getting deliverance, was a severe case of sciatica which manifested as a burning nerve pain down the back of my right hip and leg. I gave a lot of money to chiropractors trying to get relief from this nagging pain to no avail. Now, in the apartment rental office in Rogers, we have formed a prayer circle with the Moroffs, my wife, her son, and me. Stan begins to entreat God for blessings upon us, but in the midst of that he paused and said, "Mr. Warmack, the Lord is telling me that you have a pain in the butt, and He says He is healing it right now." This brought a lot of startled laughter from everyone in the room, and especially for me. However, shortly after leaving the building, I noticed that the nagging and persistent sciatica pain was no longer there. This also brought great joy that Daddy had put us together for a long and happy relationship with two people who definitely were in touch with our Lord and Savior.

Stan Moroff was one of the most influential people I have ever known; a rough man from a rough neighborhood in Chicago who was a valiantly militant soul-winner and an ardent lover of his Lord and all the people whose lives he touched. It didn't matter where Stan found himself, he was a soul winner. Many times, when we ate in restaurants Stan would always, without fail, offer to pray for the server, which would always bring tears to their eyes. I have missed Stan very much since he passed away a few years later, and I have never, ever, met anyone else even remotely like him. His widow, Violet, lived on to remarry.

THE TRUMPET OF GOD

The year 1997 was a milestone supernatural year for me and for certain others in the God realm. In the 1990s Daddy was touching hungry Americans with special graces, and supernatural joy, and bringing spiritual renewal to various localities for those who would receive it. It was a time of glorious refreshing for those who cared enough to get under the various spouts where the glory was coming out freely and without measure.

Very sadly though, only a few in our region of northwestern Arkansas were interested. For most, a little Sunday morning religion is quite enough.

One very lonely, quiet, and sad Autumn evening in 1997 I was sitting alone in my house and pondering what I should do with my unhappy life when I distinctly heard a voice in my spirit--not physically audible but nevertheless quite a strong impression-- that said, "Get yourself a shofar. I'm going to anoint you to blow it." So, I said to myself, "Did I imagine that?" I had never really wanted a shofar! After all, I'm a string player, and what business do I have blowing on something?

By the way, a shofar is an animal's horn that has been prepared to be blown through to make a musical tone. In Hebrew, the word for horn is "keren" when it's still part of a living animal, but it's "shofar" after being removed from the animal's body and the flesh is removed from it. It's a divine principle that you need to understand, that nothing and nobody is of any practical use to God until THE FLESH IS REMOVED, and that's always painful.

When it is dark and you are very quiet, and your soul is poured out like water on dry earth, and you are completely emptied of self, and your ego is crushed, it is THEN that you will hear what was heretofore inaudible. HE is always speaking, but sadly so few are listening. If it takes some pain and heartache to get you into a listening mode, embrace it. EMBRACE THE PAIN!

I happened to have a rather old catalog from a Messianic supply house, and I went to the shofar listings. These horns are very expensive, and I was quite broke, but just in case that was God speaking, I began to fill out the order form. I reasoned that if this impression to get a shofar had truly come from God, HE would pay for it.

As soon as I had printed my name on the order form He spoke again, even more clearly and vividly this time, "Get up now and call Clark Emerson." I wouldn't have had the slightest inclination to call that person, because I frankly didn't particularly like him, even though God loved him very much. That's one of the noteworthy differences between me and God.

In those days we didn't have these mobile phones, so I had to get up and go to the landline on the wall at that old house in Cave Springs. I found Clark's number and dialed it.

Now, remember I've just heard a voice in my spirit telling me to get a shofar. Clark Emerson in Lincoln, Arkansas picks up the phone and answers with his very distinctive down-east upper-Massachusetts accent, and we exchanged polite pleasantries before Clark launches into a story he's just dying to tell somebody.

Let me set the stage by telling you Clark stands at major intersections with a big wooden cross, just praying and hoping for an opportunity to tell inquiring passers-by about Jesus. Clark opens his narrative with, "I'm standin' today at the intersection of highways 59 and 62 in Westville, Oklahoma with my cross, and a young man drives by in a pickup truck and he's got one o' them Jewish hahns (horns), and he leaned out the window of that pickup truck, and he blew it at me!"

What Clark had just said to me smacked me upside the head so hard with the reality I HAVE JUST HEARD FROM GOD – TWICE! I stood there stunned for a few moments and my eyes began to leak a little. After I regained my composure, finally I asked Clark where this young man had gotten that "Jewish hahn" and he told me, "He's just opened a store in Siloam Springs and he sells them theyah (there)!"

It didn't take me long to find the Last Days Outlet in Siloam Springs the very next day. I opened the door to that odd little retail shop, stepped across the threshold, and when I did, I encountered the very presence of God almost to the point of taking my breath away. The young proprietor, Rusty Howard, was

65

standing behind the counter smiling at me, and he reached behind where he was standing and produced a fairly large Yemenite shofar. Holding it up, he said, "Sir, this one is supposed to be yours." He could not have possibly known who I was, but apparently, he was hearing the voice too!

Having inquired as to the asking price I told him I didn't have that much, and he said if I could pay a little on it now he would put it away for me until I could get it paid off, which I somehow did in a few days. They used to call that "buying on the Lay-Away plan." I've heard it called the "Lay-Awake" plan because folks used to lay awake nights wondering how they were going to pay for it.

That day marked the beginning of a period of remarkable and amazing happenings in my life and others within my realm of acquaintance. By the way, even if you are anointed for something, there is still the learning and developing process before you get really good at it. Anointing simply means there is supernatural power in it that can and will take you far beyond your natural skill abilities in service to our King and produce supernatural results.

I would also like to note that I have been forbidden in some churches to blow the shofar and have even been evicted from one for blowing it, even though we have seen some remarkable manifestations of God's glory and power at the blowing of it. I consider those incidents badges of honor.

66

MESSIANIC HANGOVER

For the uninitiated, I need to explain what "Messianic" means because it's generally misunderstood. I'd always had an inexplicably strong love for the Jews, for their culture & customs, and for the Hebrew language. I also had a passionate desire to share their rejected Messiah with them. So perhaps it's no surprise that I had been steered into a Jewish cultural environment in Houston, Texas to receive deliverance there.

Messianic congregations are those that choose to worship Jesus according to Jewish customs and traditions, rather than by the pattern of the traditional Greco-Roman church. This is natural for the Jew, but for the gentile believer, it is often an exercise in pharisaic religion that adds nothing of redemptive or relational value to one's standing with God. And that's the way it was for me during eight conflicted years.

When I received deliverance under the ministries of Beth Messiah Synagogue down there in Houston, I was gifted with a truly sound mind for the first time in my life in a totally Jewish culture. It was as vivid an experience as having been physically born and raised as a Jew. It felt wonderful to me at the time, and the Lord allowed me to remain in that mindset for eight years.

My Messianic false-Jewish identity, however, caused me deep spiritual and relational conflict after returning to Arkansas and into a nearly 100% gentile culture. It caused me to stand aloof mentally and emotionally from some good church people whose nurture and love I truly needed.

That eight-year period of false identity conflict came to an end in 1998 at an epic revival meeting in Smithton, Missouri, perhaps more about Smithton later. During my years immersed in the Messianic experience, I gained a lot of wisdom and understanding that I would not otherwise have gained. I'm thankful for that.

IS HE YESHUA OR IS HE JESUS?

As a Messianic believer, I learned that the Savior's original name in the land into which He was born was ישוע (Yeshua). Therefore, I came to the conclusion in my new Jewish mindset that it was dishonoring to call Him anything else but Yeshua, and I was mule-stubborn about it.

One day in the latter 1990s I was trying to share with one of my female co-workers at the testing laboratory my faith in the Savior and encourage her to accept Him. I said to her, "Please accept Yeshua into your life." She said, "Who?" So, I proceeded to give her a Hebrew lesson, but in the process of doing that she concluded that I was whacked-out, and I lost her attention.

That evening at home I complained to the Lord about that incident, and He gently spoke to me these very words, "Son, if you want to tell people about me, you need to speak their language."

How simple! Yet, I had failed to realize that was FAR more important than my prideful Hebrew scholarship. Even though I still prefer to call him Yeshua, it's perfectly wonderful to call Him Jesus if you please. There's a teaching I do to explain the genesis of the "J" form of His name. He's going to let us call Him that until the consummation of the age.

THE AMAZING SMITHTON THING

Now, I truly want to tell this story as gently and inoffensively as possible. If I step on somebody's religious toes, I'm truly sorry, but I must tell it.

I eventually came to accept the biblical fact that in the New Covenant/New Testament paradigm there is no longer a distinction between Jew and Gentile, but it took me a long time to grasp that. As a gentile Messianic believer, I was putting on a masquerade and trying to make everybody think I was Jewish because I ludicrously thought it made me more holy before God, and certainly more righteous than my gentile peers. I wore the Kippa (beanie cap), and the Tallit (prayer shawl), and for even more righteousness than that I tied Tsitsit (tassels) to my belt loops. I learned how to "lay Tefilin" (tie on the prayer boxes), and I knew how to tie Tsitsit, and I thought all that together made me awfully special!

No.

It didn't.

In the 1990s, we were in the white heat of one of those history-making divine visitations about which they write books like this one. The supernatural meetings that were being held internationally by Rodney Howard-Browne were lighting amazing revival fires in many places. One of those convocations was held at Holy Trinity Brompton Church in London (the real one, in England). I don't remember how long that revival lasted, but it was intensely infused with holy fire, which was transported from there to other far-away places.

Randy Clark carried that Brompton fire from Rodney's meetings to Toronto, Canada, and ignited it there in 1994. Subsequently, Steve Hill carried that same divine fire from the same Howard-Browne meetings in London to Pensacola, Florida, USA, and ignited a supernatural fire there in 1995 that burned brightly for about 6 years.

Both of those revivals lasted until about 2001, and then they gradually fizzled out. Why they ended is another story for another time and place, not here. Search YouTube for: ["Brownsville Revival, Honey Where Are We From"]

I said all that to set the stage for what happened to me at an obscure Missouri village called Smithton. There was a small Community Church in that tiny town in a cornfield, 7 miles east of Sedalia, Missouri off US Highway 50. Sedalia, by the way, is where Scott Joplin wrote his Maple Leaf Rag. You're welcome. I was sure you wanted to know that.

The pastor of Smithton Community Church, Steve Grey, had become burned out as a pastor and as a husband and was deeply discouraged. His congregation took up a collection to send him to the Brownsville Assembly of God church in Pensacola because people like him were experiencing miracles of deliverance and renewal there at that time.

Steve Grey went to Brownsville Assembly in Pensacola Florida, and he sat in those meetings, every service, for a full week. The longer he sat there, the more discouraged, depressed, and just plain despondent he became because he wasn't feeling anything. However, he continued to sit there the whole week, watching people all around him having life-transforming encounters with God. In the end, when he left to go home, he felt like he had just wasted his time and the church's money. He was angry and deeply ashamed to go back and face his people with nothing to show for their sacrifice.

However, when Steve Grey walked into Smithton Community Church, straight from the nearest airport during that Sunday evening worship service in progress, the holy fire of God ignited on him! An extremely reserved and introverted man, he jumped and hollered, and the fire of revival caught like a category 5 hurricane that evening and WOULD NOT QUIT.

Very soon people heard about the fire in Smithton and began to come. They quickly filled the auditorium beyond capacity. By no coincidence, the Smithton church had just finished building an adjacent gymnasium, and they had to move the nightly meetings into that. Within a few weeks people were beginning to show up from all over the state of Missouri, and then from all over the nation, and then from all over the world. I am not exaggerating! It began to be called "The Cornfield Revival", and nearby Sedalia began to experience an amazing tourist boom which was filling lodgings and restaurants to overflowing.

There was one motel in Sedalia in which I lodged several times, and the second time I stayed there the desk clerk said to me "Oh yaaa, you're the guy with the strings!!" He was referring to the Jewish Tzitzit (tassels) I had dangling from my belt loops!

I remember standing outside in long lines waiting for the building to open, and everyone out there literally shaking under the power of God that blanketed the property. The Smithton Outpouring is already in the church history books; and it lasted, like the previous two I mentioned, until 2001, and then, just like the moves of God at Pensacola and Toronto, it died.

The mighty Smithton, the mighty Pensacola, and the mighty Toronto outpourings choked on fame and pride and died at about the same time. That's a very sad story for another time and place.

OUT, PHARISEE SPIRIT! OUT!

I attended many of the Smithton meetings, proudly wearing all my Jewish regalia as previously described. One Friday evening in 1998 I answered an altar call at the Smithton church, hoping to receive some of the joyful blessings that I was seeing manifested all around me.

The pastor's son-in-law was on the platform, and as I approached, he stepped down to greet me. His friendly greeting consisted of this: Pointing his finger right at my face he hollered loudly... "IN THE NAME OF JESUS, YOU SPIRIT OF PHARISEE RELIGION, COME OUT OF HIM!!!"

I was immediately extremely indignant at that impudent insult, but before I could officially register my displeasure all the physical strength suddenly drained out of me and I collapsed to the floor like a rag doll. There I lay for almost an hour, shaking, weeping, and perspiring heavily. As I was struggling to get up off the floor perhaps an hour later, I heard that familiar gentle voice again that I love so much..." Now, son, we don't need those things anymore, do we?"

Nobody had to explain to me what HE was referring to, and immediately, right there in the church altar, I began to remove those ceremonial clothing items from my body, and I felt a deep and satisfying sense of relief to divest myself of them, for they had held me in bondage since 1990.

By no means am I saying wearing those items is wrong for someone else, but it was definitely wrong for me, as Abba (Daddy) so gently and lovingly demonstrated. I am not a Jew, and I am not a gentile. You, fellow Spirit-filled believer, and I are members of a new species of supernatural beings in and through Jesus the Messiah, by the power of his most holy blood and by the authority of his Rhema word. Now, be transformed and walk in its power!

THE MIGHTY WAVE OF THE 1990S

Many good transformative things began to happen to me and others in the faith in the 1990s, and even in the midst of my unhappy domestic situation it gave me much comfort and joy. I had begun to hear reports of awesome things happening in Rodney Howard-Browne's meetings in Lakeland, Florida and it made me desperately hungry for what was happening there.

Fortunately, Rodney came to Tulsa in October of the year of 1997 to hold meetings in the huge Christ Chapel at Oral Roberts University. Francis and Patsy Day had previously moved to the Tulsa area from Channelview, Texas, so I blessedly had lodgings in Tulsa now.

Things were happening in Rodney's meetings at that time that he frankly said he had nothing to do with. I heard him issue this very serious disclaimer, "I'm just trying to preach. I'm just trying to do my job. I have nothing to do with what's happening here. That's God's business."

And if you, my dear reader, think it was just laughter, I'm sure you weren't there, because it was so much more than that – MUCH more! Rodney was and still is a very evangelical and serious gospel preacher with his main goal being getting his listeners to accept Jesus as savior. I'm going to quote here some excerpts from an article I wrote at that time for an evangelical publication in our area:

In October of 1997, this writer stood where Heaven literally touched the Earth. That week I attended five days of meetings conducted by South African missionary to America, Rodney Howard-Browne, at Christ Chapel, Oral Roberts University in Tulsa. The Howard-Browne meetings and the sweetness of their fruit are hard to describe, even if you have watched the videos, and they are positively life-changing in a way I cannot begin to explain.

The Howard-Browne meetings are very long by the clock, but time ceases to mean anything during those hours because something of the eternal comes into the building, and time seems greatly compressed. There is about an hour - sometimes even more - of the most incredibly uplifting praise and worship music, led [at that time] by Joe and Becky Cruse from Baytown Texas. Rodney comes out from the ready room about an hour into the praise and joins in, and then he begins to minister to the people. Often, while he is preaching, he will single someone out from the crowd to lay hands on, and WONDERFUL things happen!

After two of the meetings that week, Rodney invited everyone who desired one-on-one ministry to queue up side-by-

78

side in long lines around the perimeter of the huge chapel building at ORU all over the platform, in front of the platform, all up and down the sides of the chapel, in ranks and files back and forth in the huge L-shaped lobby. He then moved along the lines of people, laying hands on everyone while invoking a single word or short phrase.

In his distinctive South African accent he says, "People want me to make nice prayers. There isn't time for a whole lot of nice prayers!" Often, he starts by saying over each person, "In the name of Jesus", as he lays a hand on their head or sometimes also on the stomach. Then, as the pace picks up and the anointing intensifies, his benediction gets shortened to, "In the Name!", then just, "The Name!", then, "Take it!" or, "Receive!" or, "Now!", etc. Eventually, he starts to just shout, "FIRE!" over everyone as he touches them while moving rapidly down the seemingly endless lines of people.

That Saturday, he occasionally hollered, "FARR!" over some of the people, having a bit of fun with our southern dialect. Most of the people to whom I give the videos of those meetings won't make time to watch them, because, in their religious mindset, they think it's just a man preaching. They have no idea what a joyful supernatural spectacle they are missing!

The Body does not know that our loving Father in Heaven has a riotously brilliant and infinitely imaginative and creative sense of humor, to which He was treating his people in those meetings! Some laugh but even more weep quietly while all sorts of deep inner traumas are being healed by the touch of Jesus.

Some are literally unable to get up off the floor for hours, but it seems like minutes! Many need to be assisted out of the building and cannot drive themselves home because of the inebriation that is induced by the deep touch of The Lord's Spirit. There is so much happening and there is such a beautiful and joyful presence in the building that it's difficult to leave, even if you are perfectly able to.

Hours after the service is over, there are people still laid out on the carpet, many of them still laughing or weeping. I remember vividly that Thursday evening, after the most awesome meeting to that point. It was sometime near midnight, and less drunk people were helping those who were hopelessly drunk on the "new wine of the Spirit" to stagger to their feet and try to get to their cars. (See Acts, chapter 2.)

I remember helping one lady from Little Rock who was in the lobby on the floor and was giddily trying to get up and recover her footing, but the Holy Spirit had other ideas for her. As quickly as I got her up, she immediately would sink back to the carpet in more of that debilitating but life-giving and tearful laughter. My efforts to mobilize her were hopeless, and I finally had to bid her farewell and enviously leave her there on the floor.

Many of the affected ones were not laughing, but looked entranced as if they were watching with great fascination something that most of us could not see. However, nobody looked tormented, as many critics were suggesting, dubbing it a "work of the Devil". I have observed that the Devil doesn't give peace and hilarious joy, and cause people to go on their way praising Jesus! Satan never gave ME anything but disappointment, tragedy, and bitter tears!

Don't you see? Something very wonderfully good and HOLY is happening to these people, as they will so serenely testify later. Emotional and mental scars are erased, inner torments are gone, and lifelong bad habits are broken. Best of all, Jesus is so incredibly present and real to them now!

That Thursday evening, near midnight, I finally reluctantly tore myself away from the happily surreal scene in the lobby of ORU's Christ Chapel and made my way out into the very cool autumn night. From the building to the parking lot is about 100 yards, maybe more, of a broad and lamp-lit concrete walkway going downhill through a beautifully landscaped lawn, over a concrete footbridge which spans a brooklet, and then out into the vast parking lot.

The softly lighted scene that lay ahead of me as I came out of the building and rounded the juniper shrubs just outside the front door was serenely amazing! There in the lamplight were drunken, laughing people sprawled out all over the sidewalk, the lawn, the footbridge, and some of those in the parking area, standing rubber-legged by their cars, were observed comically trying to find their car door's keyhole through tears of inebriated laughter, drunk on the New Wine of the Holy Spirit. Some of these were students, naturally prone to fun and foolishness. Many of them were well dressed, very respectable looking, some middle-aged, some even elderly. You just knew that they could not all be faking this.

A few individuals were coming very slowly along, a deliberately chosen step at a time, eyes closed, bent slightly forward at the waist, with their hands extended forward, palms up, as if in supplication. Some were alternately walking and crawling while wracked with fits of joyful laughter. Some were just rolling on the cool, damp evening grass, laughing. Some were coming down the broad walkway in groups of two, three, or more, leaning on each other, clinging to each other, and trying desperately and hilariously to hold each other up. Occasionally one of these very funny co-dependent groups of drunks would just collapse onto the sidewalk, falling all over each other, hugging each other, laughing to the point of tears, and gasping breathlessly, "Thank ya, Jesus. Thank ya, Jesus".

I am re-living this wonderful scene even as I write this, and I am realizing with a startling clarity why we will need glorified bodies in Heaven! In our present state, we cannot physically stand and function normally IN HIS PRESENCE! It's that simple! Even a tiny touch of His Glory and His Fire on our physical bodies brings us down to the floor, virtually disabled but oh so joyful!

I came down the walkway toward a young man who is a very close friend of mine from Siloam Springs, Arkansas, who with his mother, a very dignified and fashionable lady about my age, was sprawled out on the sidewalk, and they were side-by-side breathlessly laughing. Randy was recently saved and delivered from a long-standing drug addiction.

While he and his Mother were lying there, my friend, Francis Day, and I were just standing by, totally absorbed in the scene with rapturous fascination. We then saw a positively HUGE Hispanic or possibly Native American young man coming very slowly down the long sidewalk toward us in short, measured steps. If I hadn't understood what was going on, I would have been, shall we say, apprehensive at his looming approach.

On his face was a wide-eyed unblinking look of total absorption in something that the rest of us could not see. A lady friend caught up with him on the sidewalk and asked whether he needed assistance. Unblinking, and with his gaze still riveted straight ahead, he was just able to give a little wave with one hand that reassured her, so she went onward to the car to wait for him with the rest of their party. I continued to watch him slowly move on down the walkway, over the footbridge, and far out into the lamp-lit parking area, still gazing intently at something very wonderful that the rest of us could not see.

In the interim, Randy and his mother finally were able to get up off the sidewalk. However, she turned slowly back, standing on the verge of the walkway against the beautifully kept lawn, under the soft lamp light, facing the huge chapel building where we had spent the last several glorious hours. With her eyes closed and slightly bowing at the waist, and with her hands outward, palms up, she stood there in a rapturous state, speaking very quietly, partly in some other language, for a long while before she was able to proceed to the car.

Francis was closer to her and said he also heard her very softly say several times, "Look what He gave me. Look what He gave me. Look what He gave me." while facing the now-darkened chapel. This was a serenely glorious lamp-lit scene never to be forgotten. I am totally at a loss for words to convey the unearthly beauty of that moment.

There was something of Heaven brooding warmly over that patch of dewy turf on that late and cold night, something ineffable, indescribable; and the memory of it caresses my soul this very moment as I recall it. I must, at this point, re-iterate; NONE of these people were in distress, no matter how intense their experience was. No distress was evident in their faces or in their voices. It was total rapturous peace and joy, like most of us have never seen or experienced on earth. It was a sovereign touch of God.

By the end of Friday evening's meeting, I had begun to feel let down, left out, and very concerned that nothing much at all had happened directly to me in the meetings, even though I had been having the most wonderful and surreal time of my life. I came back very early for Saturday morning, the final meeting of the campaign, and managed to stake out a good seat in about the fifth row of the middle section, designated for Partners of the ministry.

Just before things began, a diminutive and very friendly messianic Jewish man named David, about my age, came and sat down to my left. I knew he was Jewish even from a distance as I saw him searching for a seat. I mean, it was obvious. He was wearing a kippa and looked like Woody Allen!

To my right was a pretty and very elegant but serious black lady who never seemed to be enjoying the service all morning.

About five minutes before Rodney came out from the ready room, which is predictably about an hour into the praise and worship, something overwhelmingly powerful suddenly descended on me and I immediately became unable to continue singing. At that moment, all my prideful reserve evaporated, all my intellectual defenses crumbled, all my characteristic dignity deflated; and I began to weep, sobbing deeply, so deeply from deep down in my deepest soul. Simultaneously every fiber of my physical being started to vibrate. Along with the tears and deep sobs, my legs commenced shaking.

We were standing. I clasped my arms around the front of me and just grabbed a handful of my shirt on each side to still my arms. I could feel the muscles in my arms, back, chest, and especially in my abdomen just vibrating with something that felt like wave after wave of a strong electric current. It bent me over almost double, and from time to time I had to catch myself from falling by grabbing the backrest in front of me. There was nowhere to fall, and I desperately didn't want to wind up on the floor between two tight rows of seats and tangled up between the feet of two people who didn't seem especially comfortable with the scene anyhow.

I began to perspire very heavily, although that huge auditorium is always very cold with strong chilling drafts of air conditioning. Soon my long-sleeved white shirt was actually soaked. I came to realize since then that it was a little of the weight of the glory of God that I was feeling resting upon me. The dam burst and rivers of tears were pouring down my face, off my chin, and off the tip of my nose. I had been extremely unhappy, and I needed desperately to shed some tears, but my masculine pride wouldn't let me do it. Well, Jesus knows how to overcome pride.

I was not the only one among the couple of thousand people in that room that something like this was happening to. One odd thing about it, I wasn't the slightest bit embarrassed. I was too caught up in what was happening to me to be at all self-conscious about it. It must have continued a half-hour or so, until long after Rodney took the podium and began ministering, and well after nearly everyone else had sat down. With the tears, a lot of pain came out of me, and a lot of love and courage came in. After the weeping subsided, the hard shaking continued for perhaps another fifteen or twenty minutes.

After that stopped, I was finally able to get my breath and open my eyes again. Suddenly I felt very happy, and everything seemed very bright and jovial. I had not felt any joy, peace, or any kind of happiness at all for a great long time. And now here it was! Again, I was not the only one in that huge crowd who was having a life-changing experience that morning. Dr. Browne is very accustomed to ministering while it is happening. [Search YouTube for <Rodney Howard-Browne, The Realms of God>]

The anointing ENables, but the glory DISables.

GOT A REAL JOB

Radio broadcasting has undergone a radical transformation over the past few decades. After I moved to Arkansas in 1984 the last vestiges of what I could personally work within that field began to gradually disappear. By 1996 I just couldn't do it anymore and was blessed with a REAL job in a product testing laboratory in Rogers Arkansas. The old time-tested "Abiding Anointing of Favor" kicked in again and I found myself in another profession for which I had no training or qualifications whatever --Laboratory Technician.

I stayed in that field for twenty-two years until I had a stroke in 2018 and was forced to drop everything, including both of my much-treasured symphony orchestra positions.

The latter half of the 1990s and into the early 2000s were years of radical spiritual change and transformational cleansing and empowerment for me. Those were the years of the white heat of the Howard-Browne meetings, the Pensacola Outpouring, the Smithton Outpouring, The Last Days Outlet, and a personal renewal that was to result in some deep, DEEP encounters with my Savior/God.

THE DANGER OF UNHOLY ARTIFACTS

While living in Cave Springs, Arkansas I made the acquaintance of a pleasant young man by the name of Scott Renfrow who was a Type 1 diabetic. That disease eventually destroyed Scott's optic nerves, robbing him of his eyesight. At that point, he was in total darkness and could not detect even a bright light. I took him one evening to one of the weekly prayer meetings that the Moroffs always hosted in their managerial apartment in nearby Rogers.

I drove to Scott's home in Springdale and picked him up in my car. Then, when we arrived at the apartment in Rogers, I led him by the arm into the building, up the stairs, into the Moroff's apartment, and to a comfortable chair in the living room. There were possibly a dozen or so ignited intercessors in the apartment that evening. At some point in time all the attendees gathered around Scott and began to pray earnestly for him to recover his eyesight.

After a while, Scott suddenly sprang up from where he was seated and excitedly began to purposefully wander around the living room, picking up and examining objects and staring at individuals in the room, first one and then another. Then he suddenly and loudly exclaimed, "Why is everyone so quiet? I CAN SEE!" We were all in such awe-struck wonder at what was happening that we simply couldn't say anything for a few moments.

Previous to losing his vision Scott had worn very thick glasses. But now he could see perfectly and clearly without them. Later, after a period of thankful worship to Jesus the Healer, we began to eventually disband the meeting. Now I didn't have to lead Scott down the stairs and to my car, because he was doing quite well with his restored eyesight.

On the rather long drive from Rogers to his rented house in Springdale, very near where the baseball stadium is now, Scott was excitedly reading billboards to me and describing sights along the way. It had been a long time since he had been able to do that. Actually, I believe he had received a complete healing from diabetes that night too.

When we arrived at his house, which he had never really seen before, we both got out of the car, and I asked if I may come in and use his bathroom before my long drive back home to Cave Springs. Upon entering the house, I was shocked to find satanic artifacts everywhere in the living room! There were table lamps with bases that were in the form of writhing dragons, wizards, witches, and other witchcraft symbols, and much more that I can't remember at this time.

With alarm right away I said to him, "Scott, these objects have given satan the authority to afflict you and begin destroying you. These things are inviting demons into your home. We must destroy them immediately before I leave this house."

It was to no avail, as Scott began circulating around the room, pointing out the objects one by one and explaining to me how dearly sentimental they were to him because certain beloved persons had given them to him. I didn't insist, which I regret to this day, and I excused myself to go home.

That night at 3 a.m. my phone rang. It was Scott sadly saying, "Wayne, it's dark again." I don't have to explain to the reader why he lost his healing that night, but Scott asked me if I would come over and destroy those items for him as soon as possible.

The very next evening after work I invited a close friend who was a very strong believer to go with me, and we smashed every one of those items on Scott's concrete driveway. It was to no avail, however, for Scott never got his healing back, and a few months later he died of kidney failure due to diabetes.

I have outlived so many good people whose lives I have been allowed to touch.

INTRODUCTION TO HEALING MINISTRY

In 1999 I was blessed with an introduction to Curry Blake, who had inherited all the personal notes of John G. Lake from Lake's last surviving offspring in Pearland, Texas. Curry subsequently revived John G. Lake Ministries in Dallas, Texas. You would do well to look up Curry Blake on the YouTube video website and partake of his Godly wisdom and miraculous experiences.

John G. Lake died of a stroke in 1935, but shortly before he passed, he prophesied in detail about who would inherit his ministry at a distant time and carry it forward. Curry Blake fulfilled Lake's prophecy to the letter, and Lake's only surviving daughter knew it, so she willed it all to Curry.

I had been serving since 1997 as song leader for a small Charismatic fellowship in Eureka Springs, Arkansas, and when Curry Blake showed up there by invitation to do his first-ever Divine Healing Technician training, and I was there, not knowing what to expect. That was the beginning of a long relationship with this distinguished man of miracles which was to redirect my life in some remarkable ways. Eventually, in early 2001 I received ordination under Curry's re-organized John G. Lake Ministries.

Y2K FAUX PAS

Shortly before the disappointing Y2K non-event of New Year's Day, year 2000, I experienced a mental breakdown due to my failing second marriage. That Saturday morning, I had decided to end my life by starvation and was refusing to leave my bed in my private bedroom at our house in Cave Springs. I knew that God did not approve of suicide, but I thought that maybe he wouldn't notice if I did it this way. After all, fasting is biblical you know. I was alone because my wife had taken another of her repeated weeks-long excursions to who-knows-where, and I just wanted it all to be over.

At that time, I received a phone call from a trusted friend who lived with his wife in a large and beautiful home on the shore of Beaver Lake, near Rogers, Arkansas. John Duke told me on the phone that he needed my help right away, so even in the midst of a rather passive attempt to do away with myself, I couldn't resist a friend's plea for help.

John and Deb Duke were solidly committed believers, and John routinely heard from God. So, I got up off my deathbed, got dressed, and hurried over to the Dukes' residence. It was a gorgeous, bright, and cool early autumn day, and upon arrival I was ushered into the gloriously sunlit breakfast room. John told me to sit down at the little breakfast table next to the big bay window overlooking the lake water sparkling with sun-starts in the morning sunshine, and he asked me how I liked my eggs fixed. The pleasant odor of fried bacon already hung heavy in the air, but I quietly answered, "Thank you, John, but I'm fasting." John Duke fastened his eyes on mine with an extremely intense look on his rugged features. Then he slowly ambled over to where I was sitting, got right down in my face where I sat and slowly said, "I KNOW YOU ARE, AND IT AIN'T OF GOD! Now, how do you like your eggs?"

I found this at one time shocking and amusing and it caught me off-guard. So, I lost my composure for a moment, and I began to laugh, but my laughter quickly turned to deep heaving sobs of anguish. I had been holding in all the agonized pain of a loveless and failing marriage, but the Holy Spirit TRICKED me into letting it pour out. God had showed John on that Saturday morning that I desperately needed help.

When I broke down, John, Debbie, and their big wonderful Irish setter doggy they called "Duke" - all three of them - surrounded me and held me close for a long moment. All three of them did! A little while later, after I wiped my nose and dried my tears, the bacon, eggs, and coffee were wonderful. After that John and I combined our prepper stuff and I stayed there with the Dukes through the imminent Y2K non-crisis.

NEARLY DEAD EXPERIENCE #2

Very shortly afterward, I prayed and asked Jesus for a place of my own, and I soon found myself living alone in a small mobile home on Beaver Lake Hideaway Campground in the deep sylvan woods east of Rogers, Arkansas. I found that place in a newspaper listing that Monday morning, and when I went to inquire about it and signed the rental agreement the very happy owner said, "Mr. Warmack, we prayed just this morning that God would send a good Christian person to rent it." I was delighted and thrilled to answer their prayer! That was my peaceful little bit of heaven in the lakeside woods for the next 18 months.

These were the most peaceful, mentally and emotionally healing, and spiritually enriching 18 months of my life up to that point, but of course with a couple of speedbumps along the way. I bought a seventeen-foot canoe, rigged a sailing mast to it with a little square sail, and enjoyed evenings and free weekends alternately sailing and paddling on nearby Beaver Lake.

Folks have noticed that I NEVER do anything in the ordinary way. As a matter of fact, some years before while I was lamenting about being such an odd misfit Jesus had told me, "Son, I have created you and designed you to NOT be ordinary." Gee, that works! A sail on a canoe, indeed! That worked too!

I got a tick bite during that time and began to run a high fever. For five days and nights I lay on my bed alone in my rented camper with a very high temperature, alternately having chills, fever, and bed-soaking sweats. Every time I fell asleep, I had frightening hallucinations. During this time, I neither ate nor drank anything. I wasn't particularly concerned whether I lived or died because I was alone and just didn't care, but I felt secure in Jesus.

On the fifth day, somebody from the lab where I worked came to check on me. She bundled me into her car, half dead, and took me to a physician who administered medications and sent me back home. The fever broke that day and I recovered. That was my second very close brush with death. One more to go, so far! From that time to this I avoid tick bites every way possible.

During my 18-month stay alone at the Beaver Lake Hideaway Campground I set up a little altar in my living room with a bottle of sweet wine, a cup, and a dish of broken matzah (unleavened bread). I served myself communion daily and had fellowship with Jesus. Even though I wasn't consciously aware of it, something very awesomely powerful was growing inside me at that time that was beginning to manifest in the most beneficial ways, not only for myself but for others.

MAMA GRACE'S REMARKABLE DELIVERANCE

During that same campground season, a co-worker at the laboratory who was a believer invited me to a Sunday morning house meeting at a remotely secluded residence near Kingston, Arkansas. That's very rugged mountain country in that district, and Richie's directions to the place didn't work out too well for me, so I wound up by accident at a beautiful home perched on a precipice overlooking a spectacular scenic valley somewhere up a steep and rugged dirt road near Kingston. I was to find out later that this was a Christian survivalist community, called Healing Springs. It was later renamed Prayer Lake.

I had seen an old van going up that way, so I followed it, and sure enough, I came to this up-scale home perched on a high mountain top, and overlooking a beautiful, forested valley. There were many cars parked outside, so I assumed I had found the right place. I invited myself inside and was warmly welcomed by this group of friendly strangers, but I didn't see my friend from the lab or his family.

I settled into a seat in the crowded living room, and a young man with an acoustic guitar began to play and sing praises to Jesus. In the midst of the worship an elderly lady in the room began to manifest, protesting loudly that she didn't like being there, and demanding that her son and daughter-in-law take her home. At the very same time, I began to shake, perspire heavily, and weep silently. That's called the fire of God and I'm OK with it.

Now, the Holy Spirit of Jesus spoke to me clearly and said, "What I am putting on you now, you get up and deliver it to that old woman over there." So, I walked across the room while the little congregation was still singing, I knelt down in front of her and placed my hands softly on the old woman's face. Then, with tears still streaming down my face, I whispered to her, "Free ... Free ... Be free in Jesus' name." No shouting, no drama, just a God-inspired whisper. Immediately the dear old lady's face was serenely transformed, and she smiled at me and looked around the room in wonderment as if she had just woken up and wondered where she was. She was totally at peace and remained very serene and quiet for the rest of the morning.

At the end of the meeting, I asked some of the people if they knew my friends Richie and Randi, and they actually did, but I found out later that I had not been at the house meeting that I had been invited to. I left and pretty much forgot the whole incident. However, Richie told me a few weeks later that the son and daughter-in-law of the lady I had prayed for contacted them to say that a stranger had shown up at that house that Sunday morning and had ministered deliverance to their mother. Mama Gracie then began to go from church to church in their county talking about how Jesus had sent deliverance to her.

102

Sometimes when you wonder where the heck you are and what the heck you are doing there, you're right in the center of God's will.

A side note to this: Pam and Ed had previously prayed earnestly to God, imploring Him to send a specific person they knew to pray for Mama Gracie. Subsequent to that they received a prophetic word that said, "God says it's none of your business who I send to minister to Mama Gracie!" I got elected to do it, and it tickles me all over more than anyplace else when I remember that bright and sunny spring morning in the year 2000 that was so full of Daddy's glory and grace.

MY SECRET PLACE

It was while I was living on the campground and after having been abandoned by my wife repeatedly, that one day I clearly heard that gentle, sweet voice in my spirit say, "Son, you don't have to take any more of this." I was never angry at her because I had very low self-esteem and I intensely disliked myself. I kept telling myself over and over, "I deserve this".

Through it all I remained perfectly faithful and patient, embracing the pain and the grief because I had convinced myself that I deserved it. He's watching you and He's watching me, and He's looking for faithfulness under the most extreme circumstances. You can do it. You <u>CAN</u> DO IT. He will notice it, and He WILL eventually reward you for it.

We proceeded in the winter of 2001 to cut that tenuous and fragile cord that just barely ever held us together, she and I. No pain or grief this time, but only a sweet, sweet relief that it was finally over. Pastor Larry Bishop's personal prophecy to me 18 months previous was finally fulfilled. I didn't rush it and try to fulfill it myself. I just let Daddy decide the timing while I abode in His presence at Beaver Lake Hideaway Campground. I have grown to hate divorce because I caused the first one, but I did not cause the second one, and I still can't shake the feeling that I did deserve those 9 painful years.

Some weeks or months after that, I began to take lunch-hour walks up a hill and into the forest behind the testing lab where I was working, to pray and to seek the Lord's will. I disliked being alone without someone to love, care for, and to cherish; and I had come to the realization that I needed someone in my life to partner with me in the ministry calling I was sensing. I was too dense, though, to understand what qualifications and qualities I needed in that person.

Although I was deeply enjoying the peaceful quiet and solitude of my life on the campground, I knew that I was incomplete, and Jesus knew exactly what I lacked and WHO I needed to get me off my blessed assurance and into the center of his will. For weeks I visited my secret little spot in the woods where I strongly sensed His presence, and I prayed, "Jesus, please send me the ministry partner I need."

Then one day I heard that sweet voice that I had by this time come to recognize and trust say, "She's ready now. Start calling her alongside." Those were His exact words. I couldn't possibly have known at that time that she was living in a city 600 miles away and was on the verge of committing suicide. In that hour I began verbally and prophetically calling her alongside.

MY AWESOME MINISTRY PARTNER

While living in Fort Smith, Arkansas in the early 1990s I had made the acquaintance of a radio announcer named Glenn, a fellow with a magnificent radio voice. He and I became friends at KEZU-FM even though we had sharply conflicting philosophies. We subsequently stayed in touch over the years.

Ten years later, in 2001, Glenn finds himself communicating in an internet chat room with a lady named Sandra in Carmel, Indiana. Sandra had been the organizer and leader of a jazz band in the old big band style, and she was the lead singer.

Sandra rebuffed Glen when he tried to become too intimate with her, so he decided to hand her off to me, saying, "I have a friend down here that you need to meet." So, he found I was online at that time and connected me with her. That started something that was to change my world.

MY DADDY CAN FIX THAT

Sandy and I continued communicating with each other by email and telephone through that spring of 2001 and into the summer. She had previously been diagnosed with breast cancer, and when she came home and told her husband, he abruptly abandoned and divorced her. When I began communicating with her, she never told me that she was contemplating suicide.

The breast cancer was successfully treated without disfigurement, but she had other problems. Due to an industrial accident that resulted in a severe spinal injury she was partially paralyzed on her left side, completely deaf in her right ear, and had a painful growth on the bottom of her right foot that had been surgically removed twice but stubbornly returned each time. Whenever she described one of these defects to me, I repeatedly replied in a matter-of-fact manner, "Oh, that's no problem. My Daddy can fix that."

During my return stay in Houston in 1990 while I was receiving deliverance, I began to learn from my Messianic friends that God is not simply an imperious Father, but He is desiring to be much more than that, a very personal and intimate Daddy. That impression grew in me in the latter 1990s until it became a firm conviction that Jesus is God, and He is Daddy.

I wasn't trying to be cute when I said, "My Daddy can fix that." I had already seen Him lovingly fix a lot of stuff, including me. Besides, I didn't want to sound religious because religiosity can be such a stultifying turn-off. She asked what I meant by Daddy, and of course, I told her but in her denominational mindset she couldn't quite grasp it yet and she decided I was a wacko. Still, for some reason, she wanted to keep in touch with that very odd person in Arkansas.

FOUR FIRE BAPTISMS FOR THE TASK

In June of 2001, Rodney Howard-Browne came to do a week of meetings in Joplin, Missouri. I secured lodgings in Joplin, got some vacation time, and made my way to Joplin for those meetings, which were held in the big auditorium at Missouri Southern University. By that time Rodney was in his thirteenth year of revival meetings and he was beginning to manifest some angry burn-out symptoms, but the glorious presence of God was still there in all of its transformational power. I received at least three STRONG touches of holy fire there that week in those Joplin meetings like I had gotten in Tulsa in 1997, and that was empowering me for what I didn't yet realize was soon to come.

Now, if you don't know what I mean by holy fire, just never mind because there are absolutely not enough words in Merriam-Webster's Collegiate Dictionary Since 1828 that can even come CLOSE to describing it. So, just let go and let God!

Later that same month Curry Blake, overseer of John G. Lake Ministries held a healing seminar followed by ordinations at Tulsa Christian Center on 21st Street in Tulsa, Oklahoma, and I was there in that for the whole week. Coming into the large main entrance of that building I saw two young women lying on the right side of the broad concrete walkway at the entrance, laughing joyfully and trying to get up. They finally struggled to an upright position, helping each other to gain footing, and with some difficulty they made their way past the glass doors and into the building, leaning on each other and still laughing breathlessly. It seemed like I had seen something like that before. Hmm. I stood by and watched this fascinating scene, and I wondered if any of it was left in that spot. So, I ambled over to that exact spot where they had been, and I found out that there was!

After a while, with some difficulty, I removed myself from the concrete and went into the building, both laughing and crying at the same time. I do both when He touches me. It was doubly amazing, because a large crowd had been watching from inside and immediately gathered around me in the lobby, hoping to get some of what was on me, and many of them DID! They had been observing the whole scene from in there with joyful amusement!

Do you believe in angelic portals? I certainly do! I found one of them out there! Again!

GO NOW AND I WILL HEAL HER

After the week of fire-filled Howard-Browne meetings in Joplin, followed almost immediately by the Tulsa JGLM meetings in June 2001, I came home to the campground and resumed communicating with Sandy in Carmel, Indiana. We made plans that I would rent her a cabin at the campground, and she would fly to Arkansas during that Labor Day weekend for me to pray for her healing.

Jesus had other plans and He refused to let us wait 'til Labor Day weekend.

During the 4th of July week in that year of 2001, He began telling me to schedule the next Monday off, go to Indiana the following weekend, and pray for her because He had immediate plans for her life, and it couldn't wait. I told Sandy, and she said she wouldn't be home when I arrived Saturday morning, but she would leave the back door unlocked for me. I had a co-worker at the lab that was born and raised in Indiana, and he detailed the highway route for me.

I got off work that Friday afternoon and lay down for some rest before leaving on the drive to Indiana, but I couldn't rest because of a STRONG buzzing & fizzing sensation inside me like a freshly opened bottle of ginger ale, and that little voice urging over and over, "Go now! GO NOW!" I was thinking, "I've just come off a very hard day's work at the end of an exhausting week, and I'm supposed to drive all night to Indiana without a nap first?" I didn't think I could do that, but Daddy knew better.

I loaded my stuff into my vehicle and got going about 10 pm. The buzzing & fizzing glory of God kept me alert and awake all night until I arrived at that house in Carmel, Indiana the next morning. I let myself in through the unlocked back door and proceeded to tour every room of that house and cast whatever unclean spirits out by the name of Jesus. I was on a mission, not to romance this lady, but to see her healed, and I was serious!

HOWDY-DOO,
I'M THE ONE THAT DADDY SENT

After a few minutes of spiritual house-cleaning, I settled down on the sofa in the living room of this big, beautiful home in the stylishly upscale picture book town of Carmel, Indiana and I began to read Psalms out of my Bible to while away time until Sandy was to return home from her appointment. I had been awake for well over 24 hours, and presently sleep overtook me while sitting there.

The next thing I knew, the sound of soft footsteps awakened me, and I found myself looking up into the face of a gorgeous red-headed Amazon! Well! I wasn't ready for this, so in my characteristically suave and debonair (that translates to "nervous") manner, I stood to my feet, extended my hand in greeting, and stupidly said, "Hi! Come on in and make yourself right at home."

They didn't call me The Wayniac at the lab for nothing. You can almost count on the old Wayniac to say precisely the wrong thing at the right time! Sandy said, "Let's go sit down in the dining room. I've got pot roast and homemade bread prepared for us."

I was used to fasting a lot, and Daddy had told me He was going to heal this lady, and I couldn't wait, so I insisted, "Let's pray!" She retorted rather sternly, "No, let's have lunch first." Well, as I have learned well enough since then, Sandy is usually right and I don't argue with right, so we sat down for lunch.

Mmm, food! I wasn't accustomed to food. The pot roast and veggies were nummy, and the home-made bread...uh, the bread...well, the bread didn't rise for some reason, but we brake it (KJV for broke) with some considerable effort; and let me tell you that was the most delicious Yorkshire Pudding with beef gravy that I have ever had in my whole mouth, and I told her so! And that saved the day, in addition, of course, to what was to follow. Look up Yorkshire Pudding online and you'll see that I knew what I was talking about.

In the course of our conversation during lunch, Sandy told me that she had previously been an attorney at law, and I knowledgeably and compassionately informed her that I didn't hold that against her because 99% of lawyers give all the rest of them a bad name. Why she didn't evict me before I had a chance to pray for her, only God knows. All the Yorkshire Pudding and bad lawyers aside, we finally retired to her living room, and the purpose for my being there commenced forthwith.

DO IT THIS WAY AND DON'T DOUBT ME

Let this be a lesson to the reader – ever since I started the habit of frequent fasting, prayer, and communion I had been getting verbal guidance from Daddy rather frequently and at important times. It was <u>not</u> always what I <u>wanted</u> to hear, but it was always right and yielded good fruit when I obeyed. So, I learned to quickly act on His leadings without hesitation.

When we went to the living room and Daddy said, "If she will submit to you washing her feet, I will begin healing her." I didn't hesitate or doubt. Instead, I immediately and politely requested a pitcher, a basin, and a towel. She had no idea what this wacko stranger was up to, but she complied.

In my Pentecostal days, I had attended several foot washings, but they were never done in mixed company, so it felt a little strange to me, but this little sheep knows his Shepherd's voice. When I knelt down in front of her, He spoke to me again and said, "Now while you're doing this, sing this chorus to her so she will be at ease with what is happening". So, I sang...

Humble yourself in the sight of the Lord.
And He will lift you up,
Higher and Higher,
And He will lift you up.

I can't talk about that interlude, even to this day, without puddling up a bit, because it was a very intensely supernatural moment, and it still affects me that way when I speak of it.

When I finished washing and drying her feet, I told her to stand and walk. Walking had been painful for several years because of her severely injured right foot. There was also a growth on the sole of the foot that had been surgically removed twice but persisted in returning. Now, after the foot washing, there was no pain.

She walked laps barefoot around her living room and enjoyed it not hurting. I stood with her and saw something astonishing out of my peripheral vision in one corner of the room. Two young men in white tunics were whopping each other on the back, shaking hands, and grinning at each other broadly. Just out of the corner of my vision I plainly saw this. It was as if they were congratulating each other and saying, "We did it!"

I still didn't understand what was to follow, but it did follow! Now try to understand, this all felt very dream-like to me, very unreal!

"When the LORD turned again the captivity of Zion,
we were like those who dream.
Psalm 126:1

BUT LORD, I ONLY JUST NOW MET THE LADY

The next thing Daddy instructed me to do was to blow into her right ear, and He told me to command it IN THE HEBREW LANGUAGE to open. So, I got very close to the ear and said very softly, "Efatah b'Yeshua HaMashiach" (Be opened in the name of Yeshua the Messiah), and then I blew!

That ear had suffered several failed surgeries, the ear canal was full of scar tissue, and there were absolutely no working parts in it, but suddenly she was hearing!

Later on, I was showing her a Rodney Howard-Browne video entitled, "The Coat My Father Gave Me". Sandy was completely disinterested in the video and was persistently talking about something else when Daddy sternly admonished her, "PAY ATTENTION TO THE VIDEO!" Sandy was shocked to hear the Lord's voice herself and immediately snapped to attention. Later in the course of watching that very supernatural video of a very supernatural service, Sandy spontaneously received another touch in that right ear, with a very noticeable increase in auditory acuity. (If the reader pleases, that video is available for viewing on YouTube.)

Daddy did many wonderful things for Sandy that weekend. He completely and dramatically restored her partially paralyzed left side. This is my third or fourth revision of what I have already written, and I have been avoiding so far telling you the whole truth about the healing of her paralysis because I don't want the reader to think less of either of us, but here's what actually happened....

It was much later that Saturday afternoon, and we had been sitting on that sofa together all afternoon when I suddenly really noticed how pretty she was. Up to then, it was strictly - and I mean strictly business. No hanky-panky, no fooling around. I didn't want to frighten her, but I asked very politely, "Do you mind if I kiss you?", and she answered very politely, "No, I don't mind." So, I leaned over and very lightly and carefully did that.

I assure you, that's not what I came here for! Honest! But as soon as our lips engaged, her left arm on her paralyzed left side began to shake violently, and when it did, she got a look of absolute panic on her face and grabbed that thrashing paralyzed left arm with her perfectly good right hand and tried to control it! As this was happening, she began to feel life flow back into her left side, her clinched left hand relaxed, and her strength returned.

Now, that method of healing ministry is not at all in Curry Blake's Divine Healing Technician Training manual, but I was sure OK with it, Sandy was OK with it, and apparently, Jesus was OK with it because he knew way before I did that Sandy and I had a destiny to fulfill together.

122

Later, Sandy complained that it was not a very passionate kiss, but I was being awfully careful to not let events get out of control. I had already done too much of that in my spotted past and had learned my lesson awfully well. You don't mess with Daddy's rules and then walk away from the situation like nothing happened. It will find you out and it will eventually come back around to nip you in the backside!!!

That all transpired on a Saturday, July 7 of 2001. That night I slept peacefully in a back bedroom, far from hers, after about 36 hours with nearly no sleep. The very next morning, Sunday, she took me to the church where she and her vocal group were scheduled to sing. While there it came to my attention that a young woman in that congregation had cancer, and I approached her after the service and offered healing prayer, which she gladly accepted. Sandy and her friends were actually embarrassed at my outrageous boldness in doing that because they had never seen such a thing before. GET OVER IT ALREADY! I have orders to obey.

After that, we went to the home of a very wealthy member of that singing group for a birthday gathering. They didn't particularly like this unsophisticated Arkansas bumpkin, religious fanatic that Sandy had brought into their house wearing a hybrid outfit consisting of blue jeans, a frilly tuxedo shirt, and an olive drab survival vest, and they attempted to make fun of me. Sandy told them that I had prayed for her and she was healed, so they dared me to perform for them. I just ignored it and continued to smile disarmingly and to be as pleasant and as quiet as I could.

The lady of the house, Sharon, had elected for a preventive double mastectomy and had a persistently seeping post-surgical wound on one side of her body that was just refusing to heal. We were standing outside on her walkway later as Sandy and I were trying to leave, and I called Sandy alongside because I was going to pray for Sharon in spite of her unbelief, and by now Sharon was actually willing.

Now, remember, Sandy was a very nominal church member who had never seen any of this stuff until yesterday, but she knew now that it was real! I told Sandy to lay her hands on Sharon with me and be my ten-factor by agreement. I commanded the seeping wound on Sharon's body to dry up and close up and it did – immediately.

Hey, I didn't heal it! I only SPOKE it, and JESUS healed it! Get that straight! I'm only an unsophisticated Arkansas bumpkin wearing funny clothes.

Jesus wants us to partner with Him! Imagine that! Partnership with God! Isn't God perfectly able to do great things without our help? Yes, but He wants it to be a family thing.

Another man out there following us back to Sandy's car grabbed us and said he was on dialysis and on the kidney transplant waiting list, and would we please pray for him too?

124

Again, I enlisted Sandy to be my ten-factor for Bob and lay hands on him with me. I commanded his kidneys to resurrect and function properly in Jesus' name. Not long after that, we got word that Bob didn't need any more dialysis and was taken off the transplant list.

Just gotta believe it and do it, but American sophistication keeps most born-again people from believing it and doing it. You gotta be a little bit crazy!

I Corinthians 5:13

Sandy had now gotten a small taste of the glory of God, but I was still too dense to see what was happening. I was just gonna go back to Arkansas and wait for the ministry partner I had asked Daddy for to manifest out of the local population. However, before I left Carmel, Indiana that Monday morning to go back to my Arkansas routine, Sandy said, "Hey, I want to do this with you." –referring to Healing Ministry. No way could I get out of this one!

Three weeks later she drove over to Arkansas, and we found somebody to tie the knot for us. It has been pretty wonderful ever since. Sometimes not a smooth road, but a scenic trip nevertheless! Two more total opposites never existed on this planet, but no more blessed partnership has there ever been than this one.

I'm still a little stubborn and sometimes I just get in the way. SHE is AMAZING and has it all together in every way!

EVENTS AFTER THE MOVE TO INDIANA

When we married, Sandy had a heavily mortgaged home in Indiana, but no income. I was living blissfully in a camper trailer in the deep woods of Arkansas next to Beaver Lake. Neither the camper, nor the woods, nor the lake, nor my beloved 17-foot Coleman canoe appealed to Sandy, so she prevailed upon me to drop everything and move back to Carmel with her, which we did. When we got there and settled in, Sandy got a prophetic word that God had sent us back there for only a short time, after which He would lead us to another place.

The first day after arriving back at Sandy's house, her eldest daughter, Gena came to visit and meet me. With her, she brought her very ill 6-month-old baby boy who was suffering from failure to thrive syndrome. Little Monty's face was pallid and drawn, his color was a deathly ashen grey, and he was screaming constantly. He had a look of absolute torment on his tiny face. In addition to this, he could not retain nourishment in his stomach, and was, frankly, starving to death.

I asked if I may pray for him and was given permission by his mother. I laid my hand on Monty's tummy and before I spoke a word, Jesus whispered to me, "It's a spirit. Tell it to leave." So, without hesitation, I said, very softly but firmly, so as not to frighten the baby, "You unclean spirit, in the name of Jesus go from this child NOW."

Immediately this baby's eyes rolled back, and he started shaking violently. Sandy and Gena became alarmed. At that Jesus told me to reassure them that He was doing work in the child and not to worry. After only a few minutes little Monty became very calm, did not scream anymore, and a lovely normal pink color with a serene expression came over his face. From that hour he began to receive his mother's milk, retain it, and thrive.

Today Monty is a fine handsome young man with a sharp intellect. He is successful in the Indianapolis business community. We all pray that someday Monty and his two beloved brothers will reach out to Jesus as their Lord and Savior.

How could a tiny innocent baby have been invaded by a demon spirit? Does that not jibe with your religion? Well, we found out later when Gena confessed some things to her mother. I won't go into the details for the sake of the family's privacy.

However, parents everywhere have a divine obligation to provide a spiritual covering for their children. If the parents are not providing that covering, the child is exposed and unprotected from some very real, darkly sinister, and unmerciful forces that constantly, day and night, seek every possible legal opportunity to destroy us, even babies!

Soon after Monty's healing in Carmel, I made the acquaintance of Sandy's youngest daughter, who wanted to meet this religious nut job that her mother had latched onto. Sandy introduced us in her living room, and I was awe-struck at the beauty of this young woman – except for one very noticeable thing. She had this huge, infected zit on one of her otherwise lovely cheeks, just below her right eye. In my characteristic recklessly bold manner I pointed right at the zit, without touching it, from about 3 feet away and I said gently, "In the name of Jesus I REBUKE that thing on your face." INSTANTLY the thing exploded, and the infection stuff ran down her face. I handed her a tissue and told her to go and cleanse it with isopropyl alcohol, and it healed immediately. What an introduction to a new in-law! And what a beautiful girl she was!

So, there we were, Sandy and I, back in Indiana without incomes or a visible means of support. I had resigned from the testing lab and two paid symphony orchestras, and she had recently been laid off from her 6-figure-paying executive position. We survived on miracles of provision for two full months spanning parts of July, August, and September of 2001 in Indiana while we searched without success for employment. Then the "911" tragedy happened, which shook the very foundations of this nation.

After that, Sandy began to sense prophetically that we were to abandon her house to the mortgage company and take refuge back in Arkansas. I was more than happy to comply because my mission in Indiana was complete. I wanted to get back with familiar surroundings and gainful employment. Sandy cheerfully came with me, and miracles followed us even on the road back home.

We had very little money left, and at one fuel stop on the way back, we needed to fill up our rented 26-foot U-Haul truck, which was nearly on empty. I inserted the nozzle into the neck of the gasoline tank and pumped two dollars' worth of fuel and it wouldn't take any more. I got into the cab and checked the gauge, which indicated full. Two dollars for a tank full of gasoline in a 26-foot moving truck! Did I tell you about that "Abiding anointing of favor"? I think I did.

A LANDING PAD IN ARKANSAS

Upon arriving back in The Natural State in a U-Haul truck, we were graciously taken in by a Spirit-filled Christian couple who were very dear friends of mine. Their large house was situated on a high hill in a large and picturesque acreage in the deep Ozark woods near Pea Ridge and bordering the Missouri state line to the north. We were graciously given a bedroom and the run of the house.

One day Sandy and I were in the house alone while Richard and Sue were out shopping. Sandy wandered into one of the bedrooms which served as an office and computer room to admire the Native American artifacts framed and mounted on the walls, and I was elsewhere in the house. Richard's heritage was Native American. I don't remember if I ever asked him which tribe, but those arrowheads and other tribal artifacts displayed on his office walls were quite precious to him.

Sandy suddenly dashed out of that room in terror, because while in there with those artifacts she had lost the hearing in her right ear which Jesus had previously restored, and she tearfully found me in the living room. I immediately rebuked the spirit that had caused this, and her hearing returned. Now, we were trying to figure out a way to tell our very gracious hosts what had happened to Sandy while in that room.

Our hosts presently returned from shopping a little later that day and we were still trying to figure out how to broach that subject when Sue went into the artifact room to leave an item they had just purchased. Sue was in the room for only a few seconds when she bolted out and ran to Richard's arms. She was in tearful hysterics, and screaming, "Richard I can't hear, I can't hear!" Again, we rebuked the spirit of deafness, and Sue's hearing was immediately restored.

That was the perfect opportunity to tell them what had happened to Sandy in that room that same morning. We didn't have to tell Richard what to do. He already knew by the Spirit of God exactly what to do. That same day he took all his heritage artifacts out of that room, took them outside, and burned them without regrets. Then he scooped up the ashes and the incombustible remnants and he transported them to a place in our area that is considered "unclean" and disposed of them there.

This is not a condemnation of the Native American culture. I am only telling you what happened and leaving you to draw your own conclusions. Sandy and I both love the tribal people of America. They are nobly beautiful, admirable, and very precious to us.

Several times after that, months or years later, Sandy was momentarily struck with the loss of her hearing or loss of sensation or motor skills on her left side again. On those occasions, I simply took her into my loving arms and rebuked the thieving devil from trying to steal her healing. Every time Jesus has given us the victory again.

One more thing I almost forgot to mention – when we got back to Arkansas, I was given back my laboratory job and both symphony orchestra positions. I had a wonderfully kind and generous friend at the lab who had cheerfully helped us load the U-Haul truck for the move to Indiana. Richard Totten had shown up that day without being asked to.

Two months later when I came back to work at Consumer Testing Laboratory in Rogers and got settled in there, Richard came to my desk with a big cardboard box full of all the items I had left in my desk those two months before. He had stored them in a secret place in the laboratory, and as he set the box on the floor beside my desk he said, "I knew you were coming back."

I don't use the word friend casually, but Richard Totten and Johnny Lawson were two TRUE friends I had at the lab who were constant blessings to me. Johnny still works there, but Richard has retired, and I'm blessed to still be in touch with both of these wonderful gentlemen.

Wayne and Sandra in 2023.

OH, YOU'RE DEAF! - NO, I'M NOT!

Shortly after we got settled into our own house, Sandy began having symptoms of asthma, and there were times that she thought she would suffocate when her air passages closed. These frightening attacks occurred many times, and I never was able to get rid of the sickness, except sometimes I would lay hands on her and command the attack to stop in Jesus' name, which it always did, but it would return again later. Daddy even instructed me to rub her back with diluted carvacrol (oregano) oil, which always re-opened her air passages during an attack, even though it left her smelling like a Greek salad. Daddy had a strategic reason for this delay in her healing that we were to understand a while later.

Eventually, feeling very disappointed in myself and in God, I asked her to please consult a physician about the asthma. Sandy went to a lady doctor in our town, and while the doctor. was examining her she looked into her ears. When she came to the right ear she gasped and said, "Oh I didn't realize you were deaf in this ear!" Sandy replied "I'm not deaf in that ear. I hear perfectly." The doctor retorted, "You've GOT to be deaf in that ear, because there are no working parts to transmit sound, and the ear canal is full of scar tissue!"

The doctor then asked if she may run an audiology test, and Sandy said, "Sure if you don't charge me for it, because I know I can hear." The result of the audiology test was that Sandy

135

had far ABOVE a normal range of hearing in her incomplete right ear. The doctor was astonished!

The fact is, we all have an invisible spirit body inside our material body, and Sandy was hearing with her spiritual right ear. Several years later, Sandy began to feel something moving around in that ear and returned to the doctor for an examination. When the Dr. looked in that ear, she saw a clear ear canal and all the working parts intact – the eardrum, and everything beyond the eardrum that had not been there before. We do not know why Jesus decided to do that at that time, except possibly as another witness to our friend, the doctor. We hadn't asked him to do it, and it came as a total surprise to everybody.

REVISITING THE SHOFAR

Daddy said, "If you will just buzz into the small end of that thing, I will cause my voice to come out the big end of it."

Shortly after obtaining my first shofar from Rusty Howard in 1997 at the Last Days Outlet in Siloam Springs, Arkansas, Rusty decided to organize a "Shofar Blowout" worship celebration on the Siloam Springs Fair Grounds. He kept records of who he sold them to, and he invited all his shofar customers to the event. A place on the Siloam Springs Fair Grounds was reserved for the event, a rented flatbed trailer would serve as a stage for the evening, and a praise team from a local church was contracted.

It was an unusually cold September day, and a low hanging overcast filled the whole sky, drizzling down a light and misty cold rain the entire day. An hour or two before the appointed time for the "Shofar Blowout" worship celebration, a small group of shofarists showed up and formed a tight circle in the middle of the fairground next to the flatbed trailer. They blew their horns heavenward with a mighty blast under the weeping sky! Almost immediately a perfectly circular blue hole began to form directly overhead. That azure disc of clear sky proceeded to spread over the entirety of Siloam Springs, with a ring of rainy overcast remaining around the entire circle of the horizon.

The Shofar Blowout proceeded that evening as the holy glory of God descended over the fairgrounds upon an assembly of hundreds of Spirit-filled believers. We were sheltered under that giant circle of clear sky which became a disc of starry heavens as the daylight faded. We all drank heavily of the living water while the praises to our King wafted heavenward for hours.

In that season we were in the midst of a period of refreshing and revival which, stretched nationwide from 1989 to 2001. There were pockets of outpouring scattered all over the USA in selected spots, but not everywhere. Only where there was a hunger for His presence did He show up!

Late that evening people began to leave for home and the praise band began to pack up their equipment and instruments, after which our sheltering circle of starry sky slowly closed up, and a softly delicate misty drizzle resumed over Siloam Springs. Some of us lingered afterward to help those who had been overcome by the glory to get up off the ground, and we helped each one of them to their cars. It was amazing, that Shofar Blowout!

QUICKLY! TAKE SHELTER!

The shofar is eschewed by many congregations and leaders because it is considered a Jewish thing or simply a noisemaker. No. It's a God thing and a very powerful one too!

One summer-time Saturday evening around 2005 or 2006, Sandy and I were due to lead worship at a meeting in Bella Vista, Arkansas. Pastor Rocky Sprague's son, Toby, and I were rigging sound equipment in a hired meeting room in Bella Vista prior to the gathering. The sky overhead had been looking ominous when we came into the building, and later Toby's wife telephoned us and said frantically, "You guys take shelter immediately because I'm watching a television weather bulletin with radar that shows a big tornado heading straight for that building you're in!"

By now the rain had started pouring down in torrents with resounding thunder, lightning, and roaring wind. I picked up my shofar, and I stepped outside in the torrential rain and howling wind. I blew the biblical "Teruah" (alarm) upward at the tempest. Well aware of the enormous power of the shofar that had been committed to me years ago by the voice of God, I stepped back into the building soaking wet, and confidently said to Toby with calm assurance, "I just shipped that thing's saddle home. Let's get back to work."

Not five minutes later Toby's phone rang again, and his wife said, "Toby, you're not going to believe what just happened! I'm still watching the weather bulletins on TV, and radar shows that tornado just made an abrupt 90-degree turn away from Bella Vista! The TV meteorologist is amazed and said, "That just doesn't happen!""

There are many witnesses to this event. I only believed God and acted on it. He faithfully fulfills His promises, every time. It's only up to us to believe it and act on it.

YOU'RE TOO RADICAL FOR US

If somebody doesn't like the commission that God has given you, just peacefully and quietly walk away. Sandy and I have been asked to leave two churches for being too radical. In one of those, the pastor, respecting my mature scholarship, had asked me to teach his congregation about the significance of Easter. I gladly proceeded to tell the people all about the pagan origins of Easter and all its traditions, and pointing out that Jesus is not the Easter Bunny, but rather He is the Passover Lamb.

That didn't win me any points, but it did earn us the left foot of fellowship. It's a matter of integrity to NEVER compromise what the Lord has shown you. And if you believe something that He HASN'T shown you, you will see how it REALLY is eventually. Don't worry.

The second time we were asked to leave a church and cautioned to not let the door hit us on the backside on the way out was because I had blown the shofar at the Lord's leading during a Sunday evening prayer meeting at a church in Rogers. The pastor soon called and asked us to meet with him the following Thursday evening at the church house. When we arrived, he led us to the nursery, seated us on little bitty chairs, and informed us that we were too radical and please don't come back.

This pastor was a person who nervously averted his gaze from us and couldn't look us in the eye while speaking with us. I know exactly what that is a symptom of. Sandy lingered to try reasoning with him while I just quietly walked out and went to the car to wait for her. The really funny irony about that whole scene was that "too radical Sandy" had just that morning called a dead man back to life at her workplace after three medical people had pronounced him dead.

The moral to this story is that just because a Jackass is braying at you doesn't mean you have to bray back at him. (Did I really say that?) Hold your peace and let Daddy be your defense.

"IT'S A SPIRIT," SAYS SHE

There came a time after all that, in maybe about 2010, that a revival meeting at a church in nearby Pea Ridge, Arkansas was recommended to us. We were not told who the evangelist was and never thought to ask. We purposed, after getting the left foot of fellowship from two lovely pastors, that we would just go in, find a seat on the back row in a corner, hunker down really low, and not be too radical.

As we were getting out of the car, Sandy sternly adjured me--she's really good at this—saying, "And don't you take that darn horn in! Just leave it in the car!" That was easy. I was glad to leave it in the car because I realized that it didn't figure into our mutual plans for cautious anonymity inside the church house. Then we tried to sneak into the building and be as invisible as possible, but the evangelist was standing just inside the building near the entrance, and he RECOGNIZED US! Dang! Our cover was blown almost before we got into the building!

Brother Bill Piker had previously pastored Oak Grove Assembly, a great revivalist church in extreme north-central Arkansas and just across the state line from Blue Eye, Missouri. We had visited there often for special events, so we were well-known there. Always when we went, Pastor Piker insisted that I go up into the balcony and open the service with my shofar. So, when these two little wounded lambs just wanting to not be noticed stepped into this church in Pea Ridge, Bill Piker shouted "FOLKS, IT'S THE WARMACKS! BROTHER DID YA BRING THAT HORN?!"

Now at this point, the reader has probably concluded that Wayne is really into himself. Not at all! I'm rather introverted really, and I don't like drawing attention to myself. My problem is that I am fiercely determined to be a quickly obedient servant to my King and to boldly use the weapons that He has placed at my disposal and enabled me for. Too radical, you know. So, I meekly walked back out to the car to get my shofar, the one in F. Later I got one in E, and the one in D doesn't blow worth a flip. Oh, you didn't know they are really musical instruments?

Back into the church, Brother Piker asked me to blow and keeps telling everybody how powerful our ministry is. Humbly embarrassed, I blushed in places where most people ain't got places, but my extroverted sweetie was soakin' it all up! I think she's cute that way.

Brother Piker preached a powerful message and then asked the people, "If anybody needs a healing, let the Warmacks pray for ya!", and he then called us up front. We didn't go to that place that evening to go up front, and I'm really struggling with all this unwanted celebrity which had lately only gained us a swift exit, but we obediently went forward, and we were immediately confronted by a tall, dark full-blood Comanche brave who sported an intimidating Mohawk haircut.

Now, don't make any rash assumptions if you're confronted by a big guy with a broom for a coiffure, because Brent turned out to be a real sweetie-pie. Then he meekly said, "Sir, the Lord told me just now that if you pray for me, He will heal me of diabetes." We were delighted to comply and have seen many healings from that problem by the power of Jesus' cross. As I usually do, I laid my right hand on his abdomen over where the pancreas is and was about to speak divine life into it when Sandy sidled up to me suddenly and whispered into my ear, "It's a spirit." I know Sandy's prophetic gift, so I switched my tactic and said boldly, "You spirit of diabetes, in the name of Jesus the son of God, COME OUT!"

When I said that, the young man went absolutely ballistic, gyrating wildly and screaming at me, "I WON'T COME OUT! I HATE YOU! I HATE YOU! I WON'T COME OUT!" At that, Brent lost his balance and went to the floor, violently writhing, kicking, and screaming. Two of the church elders immediately got down there with him, doing battle with this spirit. One of the men, Richard Gilliland, said, "WAYNE, GET THAT HORN AND BLOW IT OVER HIM!"

I was just trying to deal with the shock of what was happening when I came to my senses and grabbed my F shofar. Every time I blew it over him, he arched his back and screamed in wide-eyed terror. After a minute or two of doing this, Brent settled back down into peaceful silence on the floor and began to weep softly. He was free!

We never tell people to stop taking their meds after we minister healing to them. That's carelessly presumptive, but that evening Brent went home and disposed of all his Type 1 diabetic medications and paraphernalia and had no more symptoms of the disease. As far as we know he is still healed to this day.

Jesus really wanted to set Brent free, because He had an important task for him. Brent and his cute little wife, Beth, soon moved to Talihina, Oklahoma, and founded War Cry Ministries, a powerful church for the Choctaw and other indigenous peoples in Talihina, south-eastern Oklahoma. The last time we heard from him he was traveling across the nation as a missionary to the tribes, and ministering salvation and healing to many tribal people on the reservations.

Do you understand now how very far-reaching a simple act of divine obedience can be, in spite of all the religious devils that might stand in your way and tell you to not be obedient to your calling? I rest my case, your Honor.

SPRING FORTH, THOU SPRING!

If you will indulge me here, just one more incident when Daddy asked me to blow the shofar to meet a special need. We had met a really sweet couple about our age that stopped into a healing room where we had been invited to pray for folks in Branson, Missouri. This was a back storage room in a Christian/Messianic bookstore that had been cleared and prepared for that specific use, and we came there often. The business proprietor was our very dear friend Charlene Gates who had performed our wedding in 2001. The visiting couple just came in to meet us because they also were affiliated with John G. Lake Ministries, under which Sandy and I had been ordained.

More about events in this Branson healing room later, but we became very close friends there with Jeremiah "Jerry" and Margaret Whiteside, who lived on a beautiful, wooded acreage in Mountain Home, Arkansas. We eventually had many wonderful experiences in the Holy Spirit with them.

One summer weekend, after we had made acquaintance with Jerry and Margaret in Branson, we went for our second visit with them at their gorgeous Mountain Home estate. It was very hot and dry and had not rained for several weeks. As we were getting out of our car, Jerry asked me to come over to the other side of the driveway and look at his year-round spring which had always flowed abundantly before. He wanted to show me that it had sadly dried up completely. Immediately Jesus told me to get my shofar and blow it directly into the dry hole, which I did. What many call foolishness, Daddy calls obedience and He rewards it beautifully.

We went inside the house and prepared for the evening's gathering of believers who had been invited for refreshments and to hear Sandy and me sing and share our testimony. There was a moment about 9 o'clock, maybe later, when we were sharing our testimony, and the living room and kitchen began to be filled with a bright cloud which began to obscure the ornamental light fixtures hanging from the ceiling. Then we started praying for people, and several healing miracles began to happen. It was an amazing evening full of glory and the presence of Jesus in manifestation.

We had been invited to come to church with Jerry and Margaret the next morning and share our testimony, so we stayed the night with them. The next morning when we went outside to our cars, somebody noticed there was a lot of water flowing through the culvert under the driveway and into the pond in front of the house. Ambling over toward the "dry" spring to see what was happening, we found with great delight that the spring was now producing a gurgling torrent of crystal-clear, cold, refreshing water. It was coming out of the ground at the base of a little old spring house and it had not rained overnight. Never underestimate the power of an anointed shofar. God is SO good.

...And the old spring house
In the cool green gloom
Of the willow trees,
And the cooler room
Where the swinging shelves
And the crocks were kept,
Where the cream in a golden languor slept
While the waters gurgled and laughed and wept,
Out to Old Aunt Mary's.
(James Whitcomb Riley, 1904)

BRANSON HEALING ROOM MIRACLES

In introducing you to Jerry and Margaret, I had previously mentioned the Healing Room at Charlene's Book and Gift Shop on the glamorous 76 Strip in Branson. It's about a two-and-a-half-hour drive for us up and over the steep and winding Ozark mountain country. We went there as often as we could on Saturdays because beautiful things happened in that back room.

One Saturday a member of the dance troupe at Branson's The Tabernacle Messianic congregation came to meet with us. This beautiful and graceful young woman had become afflicted with fibromyalgia so severely that she could barely walk, let alone dance. Sandy and I embraced her together and sternly commanded a spirit of infirmity to immediately release her in Jesus' name. This woman, whose name I can't recall now, slowly got up, took a few steps, and then began to DANCE joyfully in pirouettes all over that room with tears of relief and joy in her eyes. That's fun to see!

THAT'S QUITE ENOUGH!

Upon another occasion, at the Branson healing room, a middle-aged couple came for prayer, but they refused to come inside. Everything about this visit was weird! They were Baptist folks and didn't believe in divine healing because they had been taught against it. Nevertheless, they were desperate enough to come and have us pray for the wife, but yet too full of religious pride to come inside.

The lady was quite – uh – shall we say "stout"? She was about as wide as she was tall, and her dear, meek, caring husband was assisting her on the painfully difficult walk from their car to the door of the building. She had a grossly swollen and inflamed left knee, bone-on-bone, and was using a quad cane. She would only come as far as the threshold of the doorway and insisted that we pray for her there. I knelt down on the floor in front of her and began to talk to her knee in a language that neither of us understood! I am not ashamed of my God-given gift of glossolalia (tongues), but I don't make a vain show of it, and I use it in healing ministry only when prompted to by the Holy Spirit of Jesus.

So here I am, kneeling on the floor in front of this painfully afflicted Baptist lady who can barely walk, and I'm cupping my two hands around her afflicted knee, and praying for her in tongues for about 30 to 45 seconds because Daddy told me to, and suddenly she sternly exclaimed, "That will be enough of that!"

She handed the cane to her husband and double-timed it, practically marathon running, back to their car. She left her poor, shocked husband standing there in confusion, wondering what the heck just happened!

He looked down at the cane in his hand. He looked at me, looked back at his wife retreating rapidly to the car, and then looked back at me, shrugged his shoulders, and said nothing. He turned and went back to the car with his healed wife. That was one of the strangest things we have ever experienced, and we still occasionally use it as an object lesson on denominational prejudice when we teach divine healing.

We happened to encounter that couple at the Great Wall Chinese Buffet on a later visit to Branson, and she was totally well, but neither of them acknowledged us. We're just glad she's healed and we hope Jesus got the glory. It's fun seeing Daddy fix stuff.

DRESSING ROOM MIRACLES

During my 38 years as a professional symphony orchestra musician, I prayed one-on-one for many of my fellow musicians, but I recall three of those incidents that stand out sharply in my memory. The first of those was in the mid to late 1990s when a fellow contra-bassist in the North Arkansas Symphony was beginning to succumb to AIDS. Acquired Immune Deficiency Syndrome was visibly beginning to destroy this mature gentleman who was one of the most skillful bassists I had ever performed with. Wesley, we called him Wes, lived in a city in Missouri, and often traveled down to Arkansas to perform with us.

He began to show up for rehearsals looking very wasted and pallid and feeling extremely ill, barely able to carry his huge instrument and sit through a rehearsal or performance with it. His passion for that wonderful music kept him going.

Several times I had encouraged him to receive Jesus, who could help him overcome the abnormal lifestyle that had produced his illness. I determined to be a faithful friend to him, and I never condemned him for his moral choices. I tried to convince him that Jesus loved him like a compassionate father.

One day at break time, in the middle of a rehearsal, Wes asked me to pray for him because he knew his time was growing short and he was afraid. I met him in the men's dressing room backstage, sat him down, laid hands on him, sternly commanded the AIDS virus and all its symptoms to come out of him, and I commanded restoration and resurrection life into his wasted body. I then thanked Jesus for loving Wes, dying for him, and giving him new life.

The next time I saw Wes, about 2 months later, he was in glowing good health with good color and flesh back on his frame, feeling strong and ready to perform skillfully. He thanked me for his healing, and I told him Jesus did it and wants entrance into his life now to sustain him and keep him well. However, Wes chose rather to stay in his harmful and cursed lifestyle, and he succumbed to cancer not many months afterwards.

I encouraged him by text and email during his final days to PLEASE surrender to Jesus, because he had nothing to lose now, and everything to gain by doing it. I don't know if he ever did let Jesus be his Lord before he crossed over to the other side from his sickbed in Missouri. We do what we can, but we can't make the choice for them.

VIOLINIST WITH A BROKEN ARM

One of the violinists from Tulsa that usually played with us in the Fort Smith Symphony Orchestra was James, a gentle, very likable, and soft-spoken fellow who happened to be a Rhema Bible College graduate. He was pretty much a full-time performer and music teacher. James was, and still is, an excellent violinist in Tulsa with a passion for his instrument that pretty much eclipses everything else in his life.

We were assembled in Fort Smith for a weekend of services several years ago which ordinarily consisted of a Friday night rehearsal, a Saturday morning rehearsal, and then a Saturday evening performance for an audience of thousands.

James came to the auditorium that Saturday morning and attempted to enter the building through the back entrance, but he somehow lost his balance, fell off the loading dock, and landed on his right arm. I came into the men's dressing room that morning only minutes before rehearsal time to find James holding his severely discolored and swollen right forearm in his left hand, trembling, and pacing the room tearfully in severe distress.

He had no transportation of his own, no resources, and absolutely no time to get himself to an emergency care facility, so I impulsively grabbed his horribly injured arm between my hands and thanked Jesus for restoring it to full usefulness. I didn't ask permission to do that for I had an urgent divine directive to do so. In such cases, one does not hesitate, because hesitation is borne of doubt and trepidation for which there is no room in Kingdom work.

After laying my hands on the arm and speaking healing to it I firmly ordered James to go and take his seat in the concert hall and play the rehearsal. Already having been trained in principles of faith, James did not hesitate, and he did as I instructed. Playing the violin, or any other instrument for that matter, in a symphony orchestra, is a rather athletic activity requiring physical strength, agility, endurance, and deep concentration. By the time that rehearsal was finished about two and a half hours later, the injured arm was completely restored with no swelling or discoloration whatever. Jesus saved the day again!

HE WOULDN'T LET US HELP HIM

I had an absolutely wonderful friend in the Fort Smith orchestra with whom I had performed in several ensembles since the early days, beginning with the North Arkansas Symphony in the mid-1980s. That was Greg from Tulsa. His home base was the Tulsa Philharmonic, and Greg had previously lived in Houston for a while, serving as a fill-in contra-bassist in the prestigious Houston Symphony Orchestra. I probably saw him perform there but didn't know him yet.

Greg was a kind and gentle, soft-spoken young man about my age (mid-40s then) with whom I bonded quickly. He was a nominal Christian in a denominational Tulsa church to which he was faithful, and I never heard him say a harsh or unkind word. Most of the symphony personnel with whom I was associated were members of what today we would call liberal denominations if they were professing Christians at all. I met very few in my many years of performance that had an infilling of the Holy Spirit as I know and understand it.

I myself have always been a misfit in both realms – in the rather secular and ego-driven symphony orchestra culture because I was a radical "Jesus freak", and in the Charismatic church because I have never culturally fit in there either, so I have to be content with flying solo most of the time.

Greg was a Methodist but had a tolerance for my view of the faith, and I thankfully never heard him speak a harsh or obscene word. He was a very funny man at times and would share with me comical stories about his experiences in the concert hall in Tulsa. One of those was when he had wandered out into the lobby of the Tulsa concert hall in his tuxedo one evening just before a concert and a sweet little old lady approached him and asked, "Are you one of the 'mew-jish-uns'?" Well, from that time on for many years, we referred to ourselves as 'mew-jish-uns'.

Greg and I were as close as brothers, sharing many meals and playing many, many concerts together, often side-by-side in the bass section, for nearly 30 years. In the early 2010s, I began to notice Greg walking strangely and awkwardly, and sometimes behaving in an unfamiliar manner. Finally, one day he confided in me in the men's dressing room in Fort Smith that it was Parkinson's disease, and I offered to pray for him, which I impulsively did – again without asking permission. An attack dog doesn't ask permission, and at that time I didn't either. I think the effects of the disease had already begun to cloud his thinking because he angrily withdrew from me and said, "You can't heal anybody!" This grieved me deeply because we had been such close friends for a very long time.

Greg didn't perform much longer after that and retired from performance shortly afterward. He would no longer communicate with me, and a few years later I got word that he had passed on. I fully expect to meet with him again in a glorious marble-walled concert hall in the great beyond with Jesus conducting the orchestra. Not all my reminiscences culminate in a victorious celebration, but it's going to end well eventually.

THREE STREAMS

Sometimes I really wish Sandy was sitting here at this keyboard with me because she is phenomenal at remembering dates, names, and places, but the best I can do is approximate. If something I tell here is not exactly like it happened, some of it has been long, long ago, and I'm really doing the best I can.

Sometime in the early 2010s a very dear lady friend of ours, Janet, prophesied to us that we would someday be involved in three streams of ministry. It was not very long after that when we became acquainted with Jeep and Vonnie Doherty, who had recently relocated from Kansas to Arkansas. Clarence, a retired policeman, preferred to be called Jeep, and Yvonne went by her pet name Vonnie.

Jeep was a brother to Bridget Sprague, who was Pastor Rocky's wife. Rocky and Bridget pastored the powerfully supernatural River of Life Church in Bentonville with which we had been affiliated for some years already.

Jeep and Vonnie were singers together, often showing up at ministry venues like nursing homes. Jeep was gifted with a brilliant wit & great vocal talent, and he would do an impersonation of Elvis that would bring down the house. His wife, Vonnie was his lovely partner. Rocky was, and still is, marvelously powerful in healing and deliverance.

Somehow, we soon solidified as a three-family ministry team, just as Janet had prophesied a while earlier. There are so many interlaced details in this narrative that they are difficult to cover completely at this time.

THE DAY SANDY'S NICOLE
WENT TO HEAVEN

One evening in 2012 our Three Streams ministry group planned to meet for supper at an agreed-upon location as had been our custom for some time. That Tuesday evening (NOTE!) at 6:15, Sandy and I pulled into a parking place at that Bentonville restaurant. Sandy then opened her car door and started to step out when suddenly she was seized with a startling and severely disabling pain in her abdomen. She fell back into the car seat and said, "I don't think I can go in there."

Meanwhile, the others were arriving at the restaurant. They came to our car and asked if Sandy was OK. We told them she'd had a spell but was beginning to feel better. After a short while, we went on in and joined the other four.

We all got seated, ordered our food, and began to engage in pleasant conversation when suddenly Sandy's mobile phone rang, and she answered it. On the other end of the line was an emergency medical technician calling on daughter Nicole's phone from Grand Rapids Michigan to inform Sandy that at precisely 6:15 pm Sandy's daughter Nicole had died of a drug overdose. They had tried several times to revive her, but it was to no avail.

Remember now your creator in the days of your youth...

Because man goes to his long home,

And the mourners go about the streets,

Or ever the silver cord be loosed,

Or the golden bowl be broken,

Or the pitcher be shattered at the fountain,

Or the wheel be broken at the cistern.

Then shall the dust return to the earth as it was

And the spirit shall return to God who gave it.

...from Ecclesiastes, Chapter 12

My wonderful Sandy FELT the Silver Cord break that had since birth joined her to her lovely daughter. Very shortly after this, later that same year, our beloved friend Jeep died too, and nothing that the remaining anointed members of the Three Streams group or anyone else could do would prevent his passing. With that, our ministry team was no more, but we experienced a lot of holy wonders while it lasted.

Nicole Gidley's demise during that time was the planting of a precious seed that eventually brought forth something glorious...

NICOLE'S HOUSE

Sandy's daughter Nicole had become pregnant with a baby named Nicolas who was stillborn in 1999, probably because of Nicole's drug habit. That was a deep psychological trauma that Nicole was never able to emotionally cope with, so she went deeper into her unwholesome lifestyle in order to try to lessen her anguish. Sandy had tried valiantly for all the years since her own conversion to convince Nicole to embrace Jesus and be set free. Nicole had begun to suffer from Multiple Sclerosis but was healed when we prayed for her. However, she was never able somehow to make the full commitment to her Savior.

Sandy lived in emotional limbo for several years after Nicole's untimely demise, not ever sure of her daughter's salvation, especially because of the circumstances of her death. However, one evening while Sandy was receiving inner healing ministry from a very dear lady friend of ours, Sandy had an open vision in which she saw her daughter Nicole standing on a rocky promontory close beside a tall and radiantly glowing person. In this bright and glorious vision as on a big movie screen, Nicole was cradling an infant in her arms and was looking down at her mother and smiling joyfully.

Very shortly after this reassuring vision, Sandy received a divine directive to quit her job as an administrator at a retirement facility, and she began to seek community support for the establishment of a transitional home for women coming out of addiction and incarceration.

On the day before Nicole's House was due to open, early in January of 2018, I had an ischemic basal ganglia stroke that left me severely weakened, confused, and unable to competently continue my strenuous schedule of lab work combined with two symphony orchestra schedules. Our ancient enemy did everything he could think of to prevent Nicole's House from happening, but GREATER IS HE THAT IS IN US AND GIVES US THE VICTORY! At seventy-plus years of age, I had simply burned myself out.

VERY NEAR DEATH #3

The day after the stroke was the first Monday in January 2018. Sandy was officially opening Nicole's House that day, and I returned to work at the lab, but I felt horrible, and could not do much there. I still didn't know what had happened to me the day before, so I left early and drove myself to the Mercy Hospital emergency room in Rogers. They found nothing wrong with me and sent me back home.

I didn't go to work the next day, Tuesday, and then on Wednesday Sandy insisted on taking my blood pressure, and it read 265/125. She immediately got me into her car and rushed me back to the emergency room and demanded a full diagnosis on me. They laid me on a gurney and took me into a treatment room in ER. There I began to have chest pains, which I do occasionally anyhow. I usually alleviate it by chewing one aspirin tablet. I asked the young ER nurse for an aspirin, and she insisted that the protocol in the event of chest pain is a nitroglycerin tablet under the tongue, which she gave me.

A few minutes passed, and there was no relief, so she gave me another one. In a few minutes, I began to feel enveloped in fire, and I don't mean the holy kind. It was so intense that I felt an urgent need to throw off the blankets they had on me and sit up to ventilate my body. I sat there perspiring heavily in extreme hot discomfort for a few seconds, and then suddenly I collapsed back onto the gurney, completely unresponsive, but with eyes wide open and not breathing.

In this moment of time, I knew I was not breathing, but I didn't care because I suddenly felt relief from all physical discomfort and a wonderful feeling of total peace and repose came. I realized that I wasn't breathing, but I didn't seem to need to breathe anymore. It was wonderfully restful and peaceful! I could still hear what was going on in the room. Sandy went into action, and hovering over my body she began to say forcefully and repeatedly, "IN THE NAME OF JESUS YOU WILL LIVE AND NOT DIE!"

The nurse picked up the phone in the room and summoned a doctor, saying, "I THINK I'M LOSING HIM!!" My blood pressure had suddenly fallen to 35/20. A physician rushed in and hung an IV bag and began a drip to reverse the effect of the nitroglycerin and get my blood pressure back up.

All this time I could perfectly hear everything, but I could not respond in any way, could not move my eyes, or close them, and could not breathe and didn't care. I was in a detached state of deeply peaceful repose. When I became fully conscious and responsive a few minutes later, it was such a shock to consciously return to a sick and hurting body that I drew a deep agonized breath and I screamed and began to weep profusely!

170

It's wonderful beyond comprehension to be out of the body and truly alive, but EXTREMELY distressing to be suddenly THRUST back into it. You just have no idea unless you've experienced it!

After I had recovered sufficiently from that shock, I was taken to radiology for a Magnetic Resonance Imaging (MRI) of my brain, which revealed a non-bleeding ischemic basal ganglia stroke. Most people who have this unfortunate event and survive it don't recover their mental faculties and they live the rest of their lives in a nursing home. I suppose Daddy wasn't finished with me yet.

I had to learn typing skills again. I had to learn how to sign my name again. I had to overcome some speech difficulties, and I have regained a lot of my strength, but I tire very quickly and still have some balance problems. Your prayers for me in that area would be greatly appreciated.

Twenty-one days after the stroke, I had gotten clearance to return to work at the lab, but after a few days, I collapsed on the job and had to be taken away by ambulance. I managed to finish my last season with the Arkansas Philharmonic, but only with great difficulty.

So here we are minus four incomes and living on our SSI checks, and Sandy has a divine leading to start something with nothing that's going to require a huge amount of resources to initiate and sustain. However, it has happened!

Everything continues to be graciously provided by individuals, charitable groups, churches, and para-church organizations. Since opening day on January 1, 2018, many precious lives have been redeemed and turned around to face the future with hope in Jesus. I am so extremely happy that I have lived to see this glorious procession of beautiful young women come through Nicole's House, receive Jesus into their lives, and go out to live well-adjusted and productive lives after all the horror and hell they have been through. Sandy Warmack and Jesus get ALL the credit for that, and I get to help a little bit.

BRIDGET, IT'S TIME
FOR YOU TO COME HOME

I'm trying to close this narrative, but I keep remembering experiences that I believe might bless someone, and here's one of them. You might remember that I have previously mentioned Pastors Rocky and Bridget Sprague here several times. We made their acquaintance at a gathering in Springdale in 2005 shortly after my brother and friend Francis Day went to Heaven. At that time Rocky began to ask me about Hebraic things and we really bonded quickly. Rocky, originally from Coffeyville, Kansas, is a humble man of awesome faith and is very powerful in healing and deliverance.

His late wife, Bridget, was a loving and nurturing friend and sister to everyone who ever came into their fellowship circle, and everyone felt that she was absolutely indispensable to that ministry. However, Bridget tragically fell ill in early 2020 and succumbed to that illness. She had only recently retired from her secular job so she could help more in Rocky's fruitful ministry.

Two weeks before she passed, Sandy and I were visiting her in the hospital room. That day she told us about a dream she'd had the night before. In the dream, a sister of hers who had passed years before and a niece who had passed more recently (Crystal – whom we knew) stood before her in radiant glory, and one of them gently told Bridget, "Bridget, it's time for you to come home now." At this announcement, in the dream, Bridget strenuously objected because she had recently retired to go deeper into ministry with her beloved husband. But she received the gentle but firm nodding reply from her sister and niece, "No Bridget, it's time for you to come home."

Her passing two weeks later in their home was not easy for anyone, but it was on schedule and unavoidable. Rocky, along with all of us, was hit very hard and deeply by her passing, and he asked repeatedly, "Why did my wife die in spite of all the prayers?" Like the title of the long-ago television show, Father Knows Best, His ways are not our ways, but they are the best ways. We simply must embrace the pain and press on.

Not too long afterward, a very lovely and compassionate woman came into Rocky's life to somewhat ease his grief, and we thank God for Carol.

174

THERE WILL BE A NEST IN IT

Very soon after I brought Sandy to Arkansas and we tied the matrimonial knot, the Lord provided us with a double-wide manufactured home that we still live in. But early on we had very little combined income and we had to really pinch pennies to live. The first summer after moving into this place in the autumn of 2001 we started having problems with the central air unit, but we couldn't really afford to get it fixed.

One Monday morning after I had gone to work, and while preparing to go out and apply for employment, Sandy distinctly heard the voice of God while she was putting on her "war paint", as an old friend of mine called ladies' make-up. The voice very specifically informed her in detail, "The problem with your air conditioner is in the outside unit, and when you look you will find a nest in it."

Truly, there are two mechanical units involved with a central air & heat system. Inside the building, there is an evaporator unit, and outside the building is a condenser unit; they are connected by sealed copper tubing and electrical circuitry. I called Sandy that day on my lunch hour to check on her and she told me what she had heard in her spirit that morning. Upon hearing that, I purposed to come straight home from work that afternoon and check into it.

When I arrived home, I got a number 2 Philips screwdriver and began removing the outer panels from the outside condenser unit. Due to the vast number of fasteners holding those panels on, in addition to Sandy's unwillingness to go out behind our house, and her not having much mechanical acumen, she could not have possibly seen anything inside that vented metal cabinet.

After removing the panels from the unit, I found two significant things: (1) The condenser's cooling fins were completely clogged with grass clippings, so the unit could not "breathe", and (2) A NEST! Sitting precisely on top of where the two in-going and out-going copper tubing lines crossed inside the unit there was an absolutely elegant little tea-cup-shaped nest made neatly of woven weedy stems and containing two cicada shells. I don't know what could have possibly gotten in there to make that nest, but there it was. The problem with that unit was the compaction of grass clippings in the ventilator fins, and the nest was only there for a sign that Sandy had indeed once again heard from God.

The Lord God verified her prophetic gift, and at the same time saved us a ton of money that we didn't have and a great deal of physical discomfort. He cares very much about every aspect of our lives--and yours! I have learned to trust Sandy when she says she has heard from God.

I used to have a 17-foot Coleman canoe. It was very heavy as canoes go because it had tubular steel thwarts and keelson

176

(frame components). I stored it on a rope-and-pulley system that I had rigged over my parking place under the carport. We don't have a proper garage. It hung about 1 foot above my car.

One Saturday morning Sandy was walking through our living room when she stopped in her tracks, looking startled, and shouted, "OMIGOSH! I just saw the canoe fall on your car!" I, therefore, looked outside and saw the canoe still firmly positioned above my car, in its normal place. However, I decided to go out and check the ropes, and I found that due to their weathered condition, they were beginning to fray badly. Polypropylene cordage will do that after a long time exposed to solar ultra-violet and other weather extremes. That's one of the useful things I learned while employed with a product testing laboratory for twenty-two years.

That afternoon we went and purchased a coil of good quality nylon rope. However, I didn't immediately install it, thinking I probably had a little time. Note: I'm the founder of Procrastinators Anonymous, NWA. We were supposed to have a meeting yesterday, but I decided to put it off for a while.

One day soon after we had bought the new rope we went somewhere in Sandy's car, and when we got home guess what we found? That canoe was sitting smack on top of my car! Neither the car nor the canoe was damaged, but I learned once more to listen and act promptly when Sandy gets a divine download. It could have been much worse.

YOU SAW ME WHERE?

It wasn't long after that totally awesome lady came into my life that I began to find out why Daddy had put her with me. Having just received her own miracle healing, her zeal was fresh to do healing ministry with me and she immediately set to work at it by establishing a weekly healing room. Having a haphazard nature and irregular habits, I simply don't have it within myself to organize things, so Daddy knew I needed this wonderful person in my life lest I hide my gifts.

We had the healing room in various locations for years until we were finally financially able to rent a nice room that wasn't imposing on somebody else's space. One of the places we had previously used was in the meeting room at Rocky's River of Life Church where we attended for 16 years in Bentonville. Sandy facilitates a one-day divine healing seminar at least every 6 months somewhere, and we were doing it there that day. It was a Saturday in about 2011, and it was surprisingly well attended. Five of the attendees there that day were mature ladies from the small town of Paris, Arkansas, some distance east of Fort Smith.

When we do these seminars, we try to schedule a five-minute comfort break at least every hour. During one of these breaks, one of the ladies came forward and said, "Wayne it's so good to see you again!" I thanked her and asked where we had met before. She said, "Don't you remember when we were in the

179

meeting with you at Greer's Ferry?" At that, I stupidly said, "No ma'am. Where's that?" She smiled and looking a bit incredulous she said, "You taught us divine healing in the meeting room at Fairfield Bay Resort on Greer's Ferry Lake."

Now, at this point, my tiny mind is going *TILT* because I had no idea what she was talking about! I told her I can't recall ever having been at that place. She said, "Oh, yes sir! It was you...your face...your voice...your name...the same testimonial stories you are telling today...IT WAS YOU!" All four of the other ladies were smiling and nodding in agreement. I wondered if they were just setting me up for a hoax, and all I could say was, "OKAY." Thank you all for being here today. It's wonderful to see you ladies again." ...and I was totally unable to grasp anything she said.

We continued our teaching that day and bade farewell to all our attendees at 5:00 pm after activating them into the healing ministry. We cleaned up and reorganized the room back to its original order and decided to go and duck in – a little late – on a meeting that would have already been in progress at the nearby Ekklesia Church in Rogers. Ekklesia's pastor is an enormously anointed lady whose son, Phillip Rich, was ministering there that evening.

Phil is a prophet with proven giftings. We walked in and seated ourselves just after he had begun teaching. Right in the middle of a sentence, Phil paused, listened, and said, "The Lord

180

just told me that somebody in this room is going to be told that they were seen previously in a place they are sure they have never been to. Don't be too concerned about that because sometimes Father will take your spirit and use your gifts in another location, sometimes even without you knowing it."

What he said there that night confirmed to me what the five ladies from Paris, Arkansas had said just hours before, and it sort of cleared up my mind, because what they said to me really left me a bit confused. I have wished since then that I could reconnect with those five ladies and tell them what that awesome prophet said that evening, not even knowing to whom he was speaking.

GRANDMA PASTOR

I previously mentioned Prophet Phil Rich at Ekklesia Church. The pastor there is Phil's mother, Dorothy Wall. She and her late husband had founded the First Assembly of God church in Bella Vista, and she was now remarried to a fine gentleman named Harold Wall who had an excellent spirit of helps alongside her.

We hadn't known Dorothy and Harold very long, and I was secretly musing to myself, "What is this old woman doing trying to pastor a church?" Shame on me, Shame, shame, shame! Sometimes I should be dope-slapped upside the head! You'd think that after all Daddy's work on my defective character, I wouldn't still be a JERK. But there ya go! I'm just being transparent, folks.

Somehow Pastor Dorothy had invited Sandy and me to come and lead her song service one specific Sunday morning. We got out of bed that morning and I discovered with some alarm that two big cyst-like lumps had arisen under the skin of my right arm, but we began to load our car with the necessities of song-leading. We proceeded to Dorothy's church and led the worship that morning with no problems. Late in the service, I went forward to let Dorothy pray for me about the lumps on my arm, even though I had already stupidly assumed that she didn't have anything.

When Dorothy Wall touched my forehead with her fingertips and prayed, I MELTED into the floor, totally disabled by what came out of her fingertips and into me. I found out at that moment that she has something! I lay there on that floor for almost an hour, shaking, and sweating, and silently weeping. THAT is what a touch of God's fiery glory will do to you!

By now everybody else had left, and the Walls and Sandy were patiently waiting for me to revive and become vertical again. I finally was able to crawl to the edge of the platform and pull myself up, but I was still so wrapped in the power of God that I was useless, so Sandy had to pack away our stuff.

While sitting there on the platform totally trashed, I did think to check my arm. BOTH of the big lumps were GONE! And now I have an absolutely fearful and enduring respect and deep love for PASTOR Dorothy Wall.

MAMA MARIA'S AWESOME MIRACLE

One remarkable incident in which Sandy and I joined with two other couples to take healing into a situation was when we partnered with Fred & Sherry McBride, and Richard & Sue Gilliland to act on a request to come to a home in Lowell, Arkansas where three generations of a Mexican family were living and taking care of the grandmother who was painfully dying of lung cancer. She was called Mama Maria, and when we arrived, we found her in the living room sitting in a wheelchair. She was withered, hunched over, attached to a morphine pump, moaning in pain, and of course not very communicative.

We six all gathered around her, invoked the name of Jesus, rebuked the cancer, and declared healing for her. Very soon Mama Maria sat up straight, detached the morphine pump from her body, got up unassisted from her wheelchair, and proceeded straight into the nearest bathroom, and coughed up a number of ugly tumors out of her lungs. She then washed up and came back out in full strength and went into the kitchen and served us all a piece of a delicious family-recipe pastry as she cheerfully shared with us stories about her life back in Mexico.

She was completely, totally healed, and strengthened by the name of Jesus being applied by six Spirit-filled believers in agreement.

After a while we counseled the family to cleanse their home of anything that might be a gateway for our ancient enemy to bring back sickness into the house. We then excused ourselves and went out to our vehicles. Between the front door of the house and our cars, however, Sherry and Sue collapsed onto the grassy lawn, overcome by the tangible glory of God that had settled onto the property. I've witnessed several such incidents and they were wonderful. We were all overcome with joyful laughter and had to pick the ladies up and help them get into the car.

I'M WOIKIN' ON IT

During my 22-year tenure at Consumer Testing Laboratory in Rogers, I made the acquaintance of many wonderfully memorable people. One of these was Kendon (last name withheld). Kenny was tall and thin, and about my age, with curly graying hair. He was a seasoned musician who worked as a jazz drummer evenings and weekends for local upscale restaurants and service clubs which offered entertainment. Even though Kendon was a very liberal atheist, we had a warm and fun relationship as co-workers, partially at least because I too was a professional weekend musician.

Kendon was clownish at the lab, and enormously entertaining to be with. He had a strange avaunt-guarde sense of humor that kept me constantly cheered up. One day we were standing outside during a work break when Kendon looked first one way, and then the other across the wide parking lot, and with a very serious look on his face he said, "Wayne, does this parking lot make me look fat?" I don't know whether that was spontaneous or not, but it sure made my day!

One day Kendon came to work obviously in agony with great lumbar discomfort, as he was slightly bent over, listing to one side, and had a look of distress on his face. This bothered me deeply, seeing my friend in pain. I caught up with him at break time in the parking lot and said, "Kenny my friend, I can't stand to see you hurting like this. Would you please let me pray for you?"

Even a militant atheist is glad to get help from a non-existent God if he is hurting bad enough. So, I laid my hand on his back in the lumbar area and I said, "Nucleus Pulposus between lumbars 4 & 5, you will return to your God-ordained place immediately, and you, Annulus Fibrosis, you will seal up the breech and retain that nucleus from this time forward. I command it in the name of Jesus, the Son of God!" You don't have to do it that way, but I do, and it works.

Instantly Kendon straightened up, took a deep sigh of relief, and a joyful look of astonishment washed across his face. Then he said with a wide-eyed smile, "Man, what are you, some kind of a magician?!!!" I said, "Kenny, the Lord Jesus himself just healed you. Now you need to receive Him into your life to secure your healing." At that, he shook his head and said, "Oh no, man! I can't do that." He said those words with a look of dreadful apprehension as if he were in bondage to something that would harm him if he confessed Jesus. I left it at that, and his painful condition returned a few days later. That made me very sad, but Daddy and I had done all we could.

A while later Kendon retired from the lab and his wife resigned from her job, and they moved back to their house in their hometown of Detroit Michigan. I kept in touch with Kendon by text and email, and it wasn't long before he began to have chronic respiratory issues which progressed very rapidly to Pulmonary Fibrosis, a fatal condition which hardens the lungs and eventually leads to death by suffocation.

Kendon was hospitalized in Detroit and put on a respirator. I began to plead with him by text, "Kenny, PLEASE don't leave this world without Jesus. You have absolutely nothing to lose now by receiving Him!" He would write back to me in his inimitably humorous style, "I'm woikin' [working] on it." Then I would respond again, "Kenny, PLEASE DON'T LEAVE THIS WORLD WITHOUT JESUS. He is your surety and your safe passage to the other side. PLEASE!"...and all I would get back from him was "I'm woikin' on it."

That humorously worded response always gave me a little hope that maybe he was moving in the right direction, but it wasn't enough for me. Then one morning I received another text from Kenny's phone that said, "Wayne, this is Kendon's wife. He passed peacefully this morning. I just wanted to thank you for being his friend." I thanked her for letting me know and for a long while I was in the limbo of uncertainty about where Kendon's soul went, just as Sandy had been about her daughter Nicole.

That was years ago in 2018, but then one night late last year (2021) I had a dream. Most of my dreams are just ridiculously unreal scenarios that make no sense whatsoever and are just kind of unpleasant. But this dream was different...I found myself in a huge and brightly lit room with marble walls and columns. On the

189

far side of the room was a mist that concealed everything in that direction, and out of that mist emerged my friend Kendon with a broad smile on his face. He hurried toward me with his arms extended and embraced me in a manly hug while laughing hilariously. In the dream, I began to weep with joy at seeing my friend in this wonderful place, and suddenly I woke up with an assurance that Kenny had made it to that bright and glorious safe harbor with Jesus.

Kenny's "woikin' on it" had apparently paid off! If you ever find yourself on a slippery slope and facing a dark abyss, most folks will grab hold of whatever lifeline is available, even if they don't believe in it. God is good ALL THE TIME, and He will always go the extra mile with you.

THE LITTLE GYMNAST WHO COULDN'T

One more reminiscence is about a little girl named Faith. It's an awesome thing when two desperate parents come into your healing room, and they trust you to help their little daughter.

Six-year-old Faith was born with a 16-degree scoliosis in her spine, which caused the child severe discomfort and a limited range of motion. In addition, Faith wanted more than anything to be a competitive gymnast.

When Patrick and Lori Keating brought their little girl into the healing room about four years ago, our healing team began to do what we always do in cases like hers. We sternly rebuked the spirit of infirmity, we laid our hands on Faith's little back, and we strictly commanded the deformed spine to move into perfect bilateral alignment within God's pattern for the child. When the little family left the healing room that Friday evening about four years ago, we didn't see evidence that there was any change, but we often don't. We knew that we had done what Jesus commissioned us to do and the rest was up to Him.

The following Wednesday we received the x-ray before-and-after pictures. The two x-ray shots were apparently taken, one from the back and the other from the front, giving two strikingly different perspectives. It's obvious that the one on the right is a picture of a bilaterally perfectly straight spine.

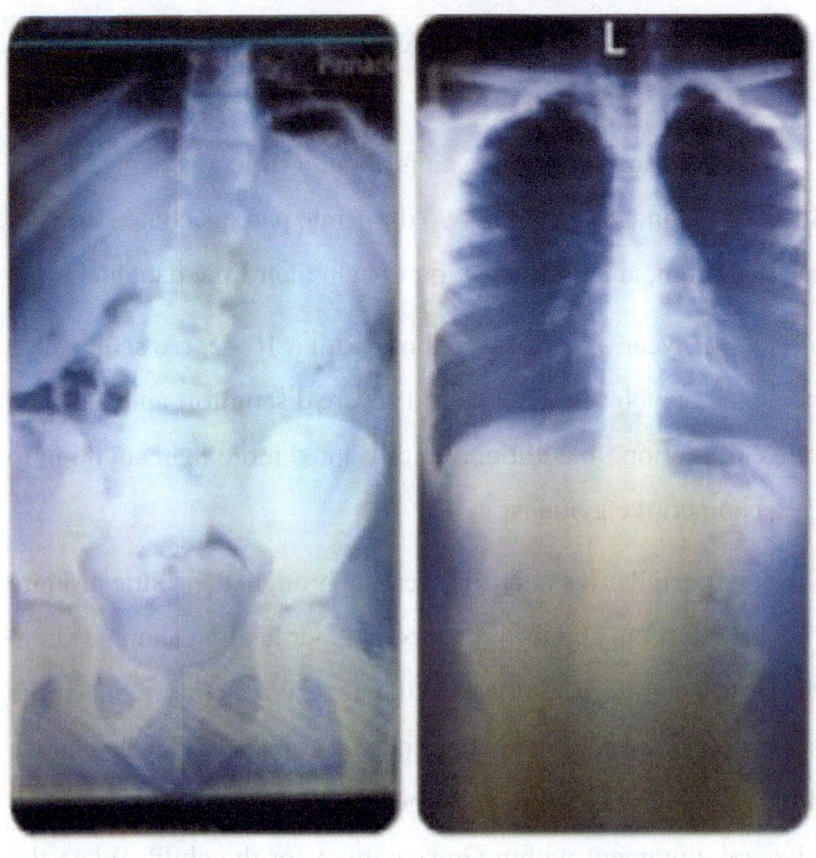

Back View, Before   –   Front View, After

Immediately after receiving her healing, Faith entered competitive gymnastics and began to excel phenomenally in Arkansas state competitions. That family has relocated to Florida since that time. Faith is ten years of age now and winning awards in gymnastics state-wide in Florida.

Contact Information

If you are reading this book and filled with the Holy Spirit you can do exactly what we do, and more, and better than we do it. Glorify your Savior with your life. You can make a big difference for someone and make your King and us very proud of you.

If you are not filled with the Holy Spirit, you can read the book of Acts to learn more about what that means.

Thank you so much for looking back with me at my recollections of God's glory. Sandy and I hope it has brought some joy into your life.

For speaking engagement contact:

Wayne or Sandy Warmack
Greater Works Ministries
Rogers, Arkansas, USA

Email: wswarmack@sbcglobal.net

ABOUT THE AUTHOR:

Wayne Warmack is a multi-talented man of God whose direction and purpose is Holy Spirit led. He is matter-of-fact, straight-forward and unpretentious. Yet he carries a Holy perspective of one who knows his authority in Jesus Christ. By faith, his obedience has led him to a healing ministry for God's Glory.

Wayne and his wife Sandy are former Arkansas State Directors of John G. Lake Ministries. They are worship and healing evangelists who believe in the power of the authority of the name of Jesus.

Made in the USA
Monee, IL
01 September 2025

23761315R00115